Martha Schwartz

Transfiguration of the Commonplace

Essay by Elizabeth K. Meyer

Interview with Martha Schwartz

Edited by Heidi Landecker

Graphic Design by Sarah Vance

S P A C E M A K E R   P R E S S

Washington, DC

Front cover:
Whitehead Institute Splice Garden
Cambridge, Massachusetts
Photo: Alan Ward

Production Coordinator:
Susan McNally
Printer:
Palace Press/Hong Kong
Publisher:
James G. Trulove
Spacemaker Press

ISBN 1-888931-01-9

Acknowledgments:
Almost all of the projects in this book
represent group efforts. With the contributions made by the following people, this
body of work was made possible.

**Martha Schwartz, Inc. (I) 1982-1986
New York, NY**
I established my own practice in Boston in
1982 and moved to New York in 1983. I
had few clients and no staff. I hired Ken
Smith right out of the Graduate School of
Design. We worked closely for six years.
Ken, to date, has contributed most to the
work in terms of design input, critical
evaluation, and sheer effort. Others who
contributed during this time were Marty
Poirier, Bradley Burke, and Terry Bahr.

**The Office of Peter Walker/
Martha Schwartz, Inc. 1986-1990,
San Francisco, CA**
In 1987, those of us working together in
New York moved to San Francisco. Pete
and I maintained separate clients which
easily allowed for design autonomy on our
own projects. The people most involved
during this time include Ken Smith, David
Meyer, Sara Fairchild, Doug Findlay,
David Walker, Terry Bahr, and Kathryn
Drinkhouse.

**Martha Schwartz, Ken Smith,
David Meyer, Landscape Architects
1990-1992, San Francisco, CA**
The flame of this office incarnation
burned hot and quick. We worked as a
strong ensemble until I moved to
Cambridge in 1992 to become adjunct
professor of landscape architecture at the
Harvard University Graduate School of
Design. The group included Ken Smith,
David Meyer, Sara Fairchild, Kathryn
Drinkhouse, Susan Nettlebeck, Jeffrey
Smith, Gabe Ruspini, and Scott Summers.

**Martha Schwartz, Inc. (II) founded
1992, Cambridge, MA**
The people in the Cambridge office
include my partner, Evelyn Bergaila who
has, with her grace and stability, har-
nessed frenetic activity into productive
effort. For the difficult and critical role Ev
plays in running the office and the home
front, my staff, my children, and my
husband are deeply grateful.

I am thankful to our gifted and
dedicated staff which includes Michael
Blier, Paula Meijerink, Chris Macfarlane,
Kevin Conger, and Kaki Martin. Past staff
members include Laura Rutledge, Maria
Bellalta, Leo Jew, Rick Casteel, Nancy
Morgan and Sara Fairchild. I am grateful
to each person for making major contributions to the most energetic work which
has been produced to date.

I'd like to thank Ann Dorman, our
CPA, who has dispensed wisdom, advice,
and guidance in the uphill struggle to
transform me into a businesswoman.

Ken Natkin and Joseph Radovsky,
both lawyers, have helped us legally and
financially through all sorts of difficulties,
contracts, and restructurings.

There are people outside the office
who have provided invaluable support,
guidance, and opportunity. I owe them a
special thanks in taking a risk on me, and
in helping me to shape a body of work.

The first is Grady Clay, who was the
editor of *Landscape Architecture Magazine*
in 1980. He is largely responsible for
launching my career. By placing the Bagel
Garden on the front cover of LAM
Magazine, Grady took a risk which, to this
day, I don't really understand. But his
editorial instincts were right, and it was
Grady, not the Bagel Garden itself, who
defined an important turning point of the
profession.

The person who gave me my first
commission is Kathy Halbreich who is
now the Director of the Walker Art Center.
In the spring of 1980, Kathy strolled along
Marlborough Street, spotted the Bagel
Garden, and, as the Director of the
Hayden Gallery at M.I.T., commissioned
the Necco Garden.

Bernardo Fort-Brescia from
Arquitectonica International was the first
architect to give me a real commission. I
will be forever grateful to him for giving
me, an unknown, a chance. We have been
collaborating on projects since 1986.

Nancy Dickinson and Ann Davis
have allowed us to create perfect gems in
their gardens. Fukuoka Jisho of Fukuoka,
Japan has been incredibly supportive and
faithful to our office.

I cannot omit from this list, my
husband, Peter Walker. When I ask myself
what role he has played in my career I am
buffeted between the poles of "because
of" and "in spite of". The real answer is
both. Since 1975, when I first met Pete, he
has been the singularly most influential
person in my career—whether I was
attempting to emulate his work, or to
distinguish myself from it. We have gone
from employer/employee, to partners, to
competitors. I have always had the utmost
respect and admiration for his work and
his passion for the profession. Without his
encouragement, I would never have
pursued landscape architecture. It is still
his opinion which I hold most valuable.

I'd like to thank my mom, Stella
Schwartz, for being such a loving mother.
She has encouraged me to adventure and
to seek my own voice and expression. It's
her humor that is the source of humor
found in the built work. In spite of what
she says, she has been my biggest fan.

My dad, Milton Schwartz, had a large
architecture firm in Philadelphia. As an
architect, he demonstrated to me, at an
early age, what having a grand passion is
all about, and that having a passion is a
gift. He taught me to focus on what I
thought was right, and not to worry about
what others thought.

Finally, I want to thank my sons, Jake
and Josie, for being such good sports when
I am traveling and not there for them.
They are the rightful owners of my time
and attention, and they have been
incredibly generous in sharing me and
forgiving me when I am grumpy and over-
tired. I also want to thank them for
centering me. For when the work is going
badly, or the supposed importance and
relevance of it pales, I never waiver in the
knowledge of how important my children
are to me. The love I have for them is rich
and colorful.

Contents

For my mother, Stella Schwartz,
and my father, Milton Schwartz.

Transfiguration of the

Commonplace

By Elizabeth K. Meyer

*Elizabeth K. Meyer is a landscape
architect and Associate Professor at the
University of Virginia, where she chairs
the graduate Department in Landscape
Architecture. She teaches design studios
and a course about modern landscape
architecture practice and theory.
Before teaching at Virginia, Meyer was
on the faculty at the Harvard University
Graduate School of Design and practiced
with the following landscape architecture
firms: Michael Vergason and Associates,
Hanna/Olin, and EDAW Alexandria.*

The Bagel Garden, Back Bay, Boston, Massachusetts

"A petite parterre embroiderie is set within the existing hedges. There are two concentric italianate squares of 16-inch-high boxwood hedge. Between the inner and outer squares is a purple gravel strip, 30 inches wide, upon which sits a point grid of weatherproofed bagels. Inside the inner square of the hedge, 30 purple Ageratum (floss flowers) are planted in rows of six reversing the purple color pattern."
  —Martha Schwartz, project description

The New York City Bulb Garden

"This planting bed will be filled first with 2 inches of gravel for drainage, 12 inches of lightweight soil mix, and will be topped with 4 inches of sand. It will contain 4,712 6-inch clay pots, each pot containing one of four different species of bulbs. These pots will be placed in the planting bed according to a planting plan for each species. Their sequential blossoms spell out the words 'greed,' 'evil,' 'ignorance,' and 'bliss'—a commentary on contemporary urban life. In order to properly place the bulbs, each pot and bulb has a specific number that places it within a numbered grid. . . . The bulbs selected for this scheme are daffodils, Greek anemone, Peruvian lily, and amaryllis. They bloom, respectively, in spring, summer, early fall, and late fall. The bulbs have been selected for their low maintenance require-ments and their ability to withstand frost and freezing temperatures. . . . The garden can be irrigated with a garden hose."
  – Martha Schwartz, in Transforming the American Garden *(1986)*

The landscape works created by Martha Schwartz are assemblages of every-day objects and materials such as can be found in most hardware stores or garden supply catalogues—clay pots, colored gravel, plastic plants, Astroturf, garden ornaments (reflective globes and gilded frogs), bright yellow "no parking" paint, lime dust, string, and tape. While some of these common-place materials or parts are not the stuff of landscape architecture that strives to be permanent and serious, Schwartz does describe her works through that discipline. Throughout her project descriptions, one discovers the spatial and formal tools of a garden designer—a *petite parterre embroiderie*, allées, hedgerows, groves, earth mounds, and terraces. It is her inclusion of the commonplace and profane, the off-the-shelf and the temporary, within the boundaries of landscape architecture that explains the outrage expressed by members of the profession as each new project is published. Schwartz's works, especially those of the 1980s, were inter-preted as transgressions of that which was appropriate for landscape architecture and, even worse, as ironic commentaries on the state of the discipline. The critics were right on both accounts. Her work was a form of built criticism and construction, simultaneously challenging existing norms and imagining new landscape worlds to replace the old.

And yet Schwartz continued, and continues, to be perplexed by the hoopla surrounding her works. After all, in the late 1970s and early 1980s, artists were engaged in activities much more confrontational than shellacking eight dozen bagels and arranging them on a field of aquarium gravel in their own front garden. "At this time, the artist Chris Burden was crucifying himself to the top of VWs, and Vito Acconci was masturbating in back of stairs, so this didn't seem like a big deal to me," Schwartz recounted during a lecture in 1995.[1] She interpreted the intense reaction to her early works as a symptom of a "somnambulant" profession, a group of practitioners reluctant to call attention to their works and themselves. This was a design practice that created places that fit in—ecologically or contextually—where they are most visible, but that usually recede into invisible backgrounds. Schwartz's reception by the profession is partially explained by this particular mind-set. But it is equally symptomatic of a creative practice that transgresses the boundaries of one discipline, or, more precisely, that occupies the conceptual territory between two disciplines, in this case, contemporary art and landscape architecture. Schwartz's act of transgression threatens the integrity and autonomy of a discipline, irritates those in need of clear boundaries, and violates the internal logic of a field.

Why, then, should an artist or designer want to do this? The answer, manifest in Schwartz's built works, is obvious. Such tactics of transgression make the familiar unfamiliar: in philosopher and art critic Arthur Danto's terms, they "transfigure the commonplace." They jolt us out of a state of distraction and cause us to be aware, to be alive, and to notice the surrounding world. For a member of a discipline whose boundaries are under siege by such transfiguration, this perceptual jolt is accompanied by an intellectual revelation that the very conventions of the discipline, which previously had been "givens," have not only been called into question, but illuminated—actually seen—as if for the first time. Danto explains this phenomenon in a discussion of Andy Warhol's use of commonplace objects:

> . . . this transfiguration of a commonplace object transforms nothing in the artworld. It only brings to consciousness the structures of art which, to be sure, required a certain historical development before the metaphor was possible. The moment it was possible, something like the Brillo Box was inevitable and pointless. It was inevitable because the gesture had to be made, whether with this object or some other.[2]

From this perspective, Martha Schwartz's projects act as a sort of gazing ball or reflective orb to the profession. They mark a specific place, but implicate larger spaces and other designers. We see our work, our values, and our assumptions anew every time Schwartz transfigures a common place with commonplace materials.

What does it mean to challenge the boundaries of landscape?
Why is Schwartz's work so provocative? One reason is the degree to which it challenges not only the discipline of landscape architecture but also the definition of landscape. Now we are aware that landscape is a malleable word. J. B. Jackson's many writings, especially "The Word Itself,"[3] trace the evolution of the meaning of landscape. He offers a new definition that delineates an uneasy frame for Schwartz's works:

> . . . a composition of man-made or man-modified spaces to serve as infrastructure or background for our collective existence; and if background seems inappropriately modest we should remember that in our modern use of the word it means that which underscores not only our identity and presence, but also our history.[4]

With their visual clarity and assertiveness, most Schwartz landscapes, such as Rio Shopping Center or the HUD headquarters plaza, are anything but background. They are stage sets for action, perhaps, but mute backgrounds, no. Furthermore, Jackson recounts how Americans have a tendency to consider landscape as synonymous with natural scenery, pastoral or picturesque sylvan images. As a society, we imagine landscape as given; it doesn't occur to many of us that the rural scenes we value so much are human constructions: they are shaped, modeled, and tended. Unlike the British, we think of landscape as natural, not constructed.

Schwartz's works, made of synthetic off-the-shelf materials, ordered through bold figures and geometries of repetition or seriality, and rendered with a touch of wit, are conscious cultural constructions. They challenge the categories of thought that structure both the profession and popular culture's definitions of landscape: natural versus cultural, enduring versus temporary, real versus synthetic, serious versus ironic, and background versus foreground. This challenge to the definition of landscape raises the stakes for landscape architecture. Not content to form a background to life and art, but aspiring to represent life and art through the landscape, Schwartz's works resonate with an idea of landscape posited by two British geographers, Denis Cosgrove and Stephen Daniels. They write:

> Landscape is a cultural image, a pictorial way of representing, structuring or symbolizing surroundings. This is not to say that landscapes are immaterial. They may be represented in a variety of materials and on many surfaces—in paint on canvas, in writing on paper, in earth, stone, water, and vegetation on the ground.[5]

Schwartz's built projects call on the landscape to do more than accommodate function. The spaces and forms of the landscape should also represent, embody, and symbolize how one sees the world.

Challenges to late-20th-century practices of landscape

Danto suggests that Warhol's series of Brillo boxes illuminate the normative structures by which art was defined and criticized in the 1960s. Schwartz's pop landscapes have the same effect. They illuminate the structures and strictures through which landscape architects define the types of projects they conceive, the sorts of sites worthy of their attention, and the design principles they employ. What are the challenges to these structural assumptions? The first is fundamental—that landscape architects are engaged in a practice that is as enmeshed in the cultural as it is the natural, the artificial as much as the real. Humans live in and imagine the world through a cultural lens; we value landscapes, nature, and the wild because of their roles in our culture. In other words, we are not generally working with some version of an undefiled, untampered nature. The second challenge addresses how blinded many landscape architects are to the pervasiveness of vernacular, suburban, and industrial landscapes, and how these shaped spaces may provide source material and inspiration for a designer. Rather than turning away from these landscapes of asphalt, speculative development, inexpensive construction, and questionable taste, one might recognize their influence on popular culture. Projects like the Columbus Convention Center and the Center for Innovative Technology embrace the spatial types and actual materials of the found landscapes of suburbia, the strip, and the parking lot.

The third challenge to the profession is related to the second. There is a tendency to limit landscape architecture's scope to spaces worthy of the pursuit: urban parks, corporate headquarters and plazas, fine gardens, campuses, and so on. One shouldn't waste energies on less prestigious spaces: the parking lot, the median strip, the highway right-of-way, the residual space between buildings, the marginal places within buildings. Those areas are abandoned or neglected by both their owners and many landscape architects. Consequently, their character is the unintended consequence of other decisions or the result of an engineer's hand. Schwartz sees these spaces as not only significant but vital to the profession, given the small number of the prestigious project types and the ubiquitousness of the other. The Citadel, Whitehead Institute, and Miami International Airport commissions all capitalize on spaces deemed invisible or inconsequential by others, and in doing so they help to make places out of otherwise alienating territories.

Finally, Schwartz's palette of materials evokes neither spaces of nature nor refined taste. Instead of a long list of trees, shrubs, perennials, thermal granite surfaces, and hand-crafted railings, one finds stamped colored concrete, Bomanite, asphalt, utility paint, concrete masonry units, fiberglass, Astroturf, Plexiglas, traffic barriers, railroad rails and ties, tires, and other ready-made or off-the-shelf items. This lack of refinement, this embracing of common (as in readily available and crass) materials, offends some who associate these items with tacky suburban gardens or industrial spaces. Schwartz counters with an argument that these are the available and inexpensive materials of the building industry. Why not try to make something honest and beautiful with them? Why not try to transfigure the commonplace? The pragmatism and populism of this approach is often obscured by debates about style and beauty. If Danto is correct in his contention that beauty "may not have a descriptive value,"[6] but may be encoded in one's relationship to the world and may be a "function of what one's beliefs about an object are,"[7] then we might attend to the reasons why we don't value these materials and items. Those biases and prejudices may be limiting our ability to create new landscape worlds or to imagine new forms of the beautiful.

In addition to the challenges to the discipline and profession of landscape architecture, Schwartz's practice confronts the profession of architecture and its marginalization of landscape as a subject and a space. This rhetorical challenge is currently being tested through the redesign of three plazas associated with examples of late modern architecture, the Federal Courthouse in Minneapolis, the U.S. Department of Housing and Urban Development (HUD) headquarters in Washington, D.C., by Marcel Breuer, and the Jacob Javits federal building in New York City, until recently the site of Richard Serra's "Tilted Arc." These specific proposals are built critiques of modern architecture's repression of the landscape and its relegation of landscape to an open space, a tabula rasa, a podium for a sculptural, object building. In lieu of this impoverished role, Schwartz presents architecture with a new set of conventions for landscape. These include the recognition that we live in space, both interior and exterior, and that design cannot stop at the building wall; that a building is only one object in a still life of many objects; that the landscape as well as architecture has not only form but content; and that space is full, not open, before an architecture is called to action. Schwartz is as aggressive in her reworkings of these tough urban spaces as the architects who preceded her. In Washington, D.C., the HUD headquarters, designed by Breuer in the 1960s, epitomizes the urban sensibilities of that period. This X-shaped concrete building is elevated on pilotis in the center of a 6-acre unarticulated parcel. Schwartz's proposal calls for not only reasserting the public realm through a three-dimensional carpet of circular plant beds and seat walls covered by colorful vinyl disks to create shade, but also suggests demolishing part of the ground floor of the building in order to create connections between the four unrelated quadrants of the parcel. In New York City, where contemporary urban landscape design can be reduced to selecting stock items from the Parks Department's list of appropriate materials, such as World's Fair benches, Central Park light standards, cast-iron hoop edging, granite seats, and bluestone pavers, Schwartz is adopting another strategy for objectifying the public realm. Playing by the rules, Schwartz's design proposal for the Jacob Javits plaza includes, in her words, "traditional New York park elements with a humorous twist."[8] These elements are transfigured not only through their dimensional distortions (light standards attenuate from 12 to 30 feet high), but also through their assemblage and alignment. For instance, the standard wood slat benches are aligned in long reverse curves that create a pattern not unlike the scroll and knot *embroiderie* within a French garden parterre. Through her hybridizing of park furniture and garden plans, Schwartz introduces Gilmore Clarke to André Le Nôtre. The result is a design that speaks of its own time, while quoting from its past without resorting to the generic contextualism of so many other recent New York City public landscapes. A final example of this aggressive stance toward a preexisting architectural space is her proclivity to work the vertical as well as the horizontal surface. Both the temporary Turf Parterre garden at Battery Park City and the Whitehead Institute Splice Garden in Cambridge, Massachusetts, continue patterns and gestures from the ground to the wall, the horizontal to the vertical, transgressing the limits of construction and scope deemed fitting for a landscape architect.

Martha Schwartz's work as it exemplifies a postmodern practice

This tendency to challenge the conceptual boundaries of a discipline is a characteristic of many cultural practices in the later decades of the 20th century. In this light, Schwartz is a typical postmodernist. She has found moments for invention on the edges or margins of two fields, at the intersection of public art and landscape architecture. Furthermore, by ironically folding images and materials from mass culture into her works, Schwartz has defied what cultural critic Andreas Huyssen called the "great divide" between high art and mass culture and, in doing so, solidifies her position as a postmodernist.[9] Yet Schwartz situates herself and her work within a modern framework. A formal analysis of her work confirms this. Pure geometric spaces and shapes such as squares, circles, and ellipses float atop fields made taut by repetitive meters. Grids and their three-dimensional extrusion, boxes, are animated by their juxtaposition with overscaled objects. The ordering devices of abstract art and minimal art are appropriated and applied to the landscape realm. It is this application of modern formal devices to a new context, within a new conceptual field that includes that which was previously excluded, that Huyssen suggests is the mark of a postmodern practice. Schwartz's work embodies both a continuation of the modern and a critique of it, both the embracing of modern art's formal principles and the irreverent employment of those

strategies in a new arena. This theoretical perspective allows us to see Schwartz as more than a renegade in the profession of landscape architecture. It redefines her, and works of landscape architecture, as active participants in a broader creative and cultural realm. It defines landscape architecture as a cultural practice as well as a profession.

This reading of Schwartz as a postmodern cultural practitioner who seeks to reinvigorate the modern through contamination and reinscription offers an alternative to the conservative mode of postmodern practice that rejects modernity and substitutes a mode of historicism or contextualism. Like kindred spirits in art and architecture such as Warhol and Robert Venturi or Rem Koolhaas, Schwartz has looked to the commercial market, mass culture, the strip, and the suburb for sources of content and contamination. She has inscribed those influences into a new field: the art and practice of gardens and landscape. Therein lies her uniqueness.

Martha Schwartz as an insider and outsider

Despite these connections to contemporary art practices, to camps within the architecture profession and to broader postmodern cultural practices, Martha Schwartz has few kindred spirits in contemporary landscape architecture. Yet, despite this immersion in the discourses of other fields, Schwartz's works are identified with the traditions of landscape architecture and the craft of garden-making. Because the parts that she assembles to construct her visions are parterres, topiaries, and bosques, the work confronts. Because of the associations of her landscape forms with vernacular and high garden ornament, the work offends. In fact, it is the strong connection to the history and traditions of both landscape architecture *and* art that creates the power of Schwartz's work. Otherwise, she would be simply one more artist expanding her scope into a new field, but oblivious to its traditions—another Mary Miss or Elyn Zimmerman. Instead, Schwartz's explicit references to the traditions of garden-making situate her firmly within both art and landscape design, and at the intersection between them.

What are these connections to the traditions of landscape architecture? Of course, there is the extraction and distortion of parts of the 17th-century French garden in projects like the Bagel Garden, the Necco Garden, the Whitehead Institute Splice Garden, and the King County Jailhouse Garden. These compartments, *embroiderie* and parterres, might be as credibly described by Antoine-Joseph d'Argenville Dezallier in his treatise, *La Théorie et la Practique du Jardinage* (1709) as by a late-20th-century artist.[10] This French garden treatise describes the practices of designing a parterre, laying it out on paper with drafting tools, and then transferring that design to the ground with stakes and string, techniques recalled in photographic documentation of the temporary Necco Garden installation on the MIT campus. The invention that is coupled with these self-conscious historical quotations revolves around the rendering of these forms with unexpected materials—plastic, tires, candies, and shattered ceramic tile work. Making the familiar unfamiliar. Transfiguring the Commonplace.

At times, the garden forms evoke associations that baffle both owner and critic. What are we to make of the gilded frogs gazing at the wire-frame globe at Rio Shopping Center? Perhaps they are the cheapest garden ornaments available in suburban Atlanta. But, given their location in a water basin and their radiating relationship to the dominant orb, one is tempted to make comparisons with the Latona Fountain at Versailles, where a group of open-mouthed frogs perch on concentric stone copings. The central statue, elevated above the circular water basins and the frogs, is of Latona and Jupiter's children, Diana and Apollo, the future "sun king."[11] According to myth, the frogs are actually peasants whom the god Jupiter metamorphosed into lowly amphibians because of their disrespectful mocking of Latona and Jupiter's children. Who has been mocking Schwartz, and why are they condemned to a lifetime of worshipping the kudzu globe? Or, who is Schwartz mocking here? The critics who say this isn't landscape architecture, and who don't know their own history well enough to appreciate a good garden joke when they see one?

Other aspects of Schwartz's work, such has her roof gardens, connect her to early-20th-century designers such as Guévrekian and Le Corbusier. In particular, the surrealism and objectification of nature at the Splice Garden recall garden design experiments from the 1920s and 1930s. Guévrekian's terrace garden at the Villa Noailles in Hyères, France, was an icon for early modernist landscape architects. Fletcher Steele's publication of that garden in the American press jolted the profession out of its Beaux Arts complacency. Besides sharing its shock-value role with the Schwartz roof gardens, the Guévrekian garden also explores the relationship between perceptual and conceptual ordering in its distortion of the ground plane and its associated perspectival structure. The result is a surface that vacillates between the horizontal and the vertical, that engages the garden visitor in optical and perceptual play. This tactic is applied at the Splice Garden, where both the Astroturf surface and the topiaries jump from ground to wall to roof ledge. This surreal aspect of the Splice Garden, in which forms assume exaggerated dimensions and odd locations, comes close to the play encountered at one of Le Corbusier's Beistegui roof gardens in Paris.

The third reference for contextualizing Schwartz's work within the traditions of garden and landscape making involves her recent tendency to figure the ground plane through the sculptural shaping of the earth. While it is tempting to mention Noguchi, Smithson, and Heizer as precursors, one shouldn't ignore the traditions of Japanese mound building, or the contemporary explorations of James Rose, Garrett Eckbo, and A.E. Bye as related inquiries. Schwartz's emphatic sculptural earth gestures are all the more powerful because of their siting on surfaces deemed invisible by contemporary architecture. The Minneapolis Federal Courthouse plaza is scaled and figured with a swarm of elliptical drumlin mounds that both establish a grain for movement and a secondary scaling device for the plaza. In Schwartz's plan for the Rem Koolhaas Kunsthal Museumpark in Rotterdam, she figures the horizontal plane into a shiny black elliptical mound emerging out of a large water basin. There, Koolhaas's interest in scaling, and the juxtaposition of scales within the contemporary urban environment, is accompanied by an assertive, sculptural landscape presence. At the World Trade Towers Plaza, circular depressions acknowledge the impossibility of making a landscape object or objects to hold these giants. So the plan is articulated in the subtlest of sectional cuts—a series of subtractive dishes sculpted into the plaza surface, imperceptible except when filled with water. Then they constitute a field of pools evenly distributed across the plaza.

Two projects extend this figuring of the ground plane into the symbolic dimension. The most recent, the West Shore and Rash Field Park in Baltimore, includes an undulating grassy field intersected by narrow paths. When viewed as a set, the individual mounds congeal into the shape of a blue crab, a delicacy for which Baltimore and the Chesapeake Bay are well known. Bordering on kitsch, this earthen crab references the local culture, an icon popularly associated with the region. Destined to become an insider's joke, known to the community and pointed out from airplane windows as one flies over the Inner Harbor, the blue crab manages to make a place, to rescue the landscape from a condition of invisibility and open space. Less witty but equally referential is the elongated loaf-shaped mound that Schwartz proposed for the Holocaust Memorial Competition in Boston. This 350-foot-long, 12-foot-high concrete block mound is simultaneously of the earth and industrial in character. The lumpen shape seems to emerge from the ground itself, a narrow medium assaulted by cars and tourists. Yet the wholeness of the memorial is denied by its construction out of small units, thousands of them. It is simultaneously Etruscan burial mound and concentration camp oven, place of rest and unrest, cemetery and incinerator. It is one thing, it is a multiplicity of singularities. It is a site of horror, a postmodern version of the sublime. The project resonates with meanings, offered up because of the images familiar to us from mass culture as well as the forms and typologies familiar to us through landscape history.

The power of Martha Schwartz's built and speculative landscapes is a function of their hybrid nature. Her projects are replete with references, formal and iconographic, to the conventions and traditions of garden-making. Yet they are imagined through the eyes and hands of an artist and a consumer of mass culture who sees value and meaning in the ready-made, the mass-produced, and the off-the-shelf.

Landscapes as symbols and images

Martha Schwartz's work raises questions about how and to whom landscapes communicate. Given her multiple allegiances to the discourses of art and landscape architecture, to mass culture as well as high art, to the permanent and the temporary, the witty and the profound, it's not surprising that the work is difficult to decipher. As this essay has attempted to show through a few examples, the act of interpretation is worth the effort. For those within the field of landscape architecture, this body of work, just now reaching professional maturity, "offers itself as a mirror."[12] In that surface is reflected the formlessness and shallowness of much of the profession. Schwartz's work is not simply trying to make the landscape visible, it is reinvigorating it with meaning. For those in the field of architecture, Schwartz's landscape works resist the impulse to assume an empty site, to clear the site prior to designing. Her projects require architects to open up their buildings to communication with their surroundings and, most directly, with their ground plane, the surface upon which life occurs. And for those outside these two design fields, Schwartz's messy position between art and landscape architecture reveals how hollow much work is that purports to blur the boundaries of a discipline. In comparison, much of this work is a form of disciplinary colonization, a settling into the territory of another without knowledge of its traditions, conventions, languages, or customs. Schwartz's work offers an alternative, a hybrid activity that draws meaning and forms from two bodies of thought and practice with the intention of neither transforming one discipline nor redirecting the other. It adopts this difficult position as a means to redefine the role and the meaning of landscape in a consumer culture.

A project designed by Martha Schwartz and her colleagues doesn't simply challenge our eyes: it challenges our minds. As Danto summarizes the function of those Brillo boxes, so too can we reconsider those landscapes of bagels, Neccos, gilded frogs, Astroturf parterres, morphed New York City lights and benches, and earthen crabs. "It does what works of art have always done—externalizing a way of viewing the world, expressing the interior of a cultural period, offering itself as a mirror to catch the conscience of our kings."[13] For other landscape architects, Schwartz's projects highlight the conceptual structures through which we define our discipline. They throw light on current limits and point out new directions or possibilities.

Martha Schwartz has said that not all works have to be masterpieces—enduring, timeless, and revered. What does she mean by that? It may be enough for certain works to be vehicles for re-presenting landscape to a community, a client, a consultant. This idea of design propositions as re-presentation, as a re-viewing box or late-20th-century *claude glass*, establishes a framework for appreciating temporary works, commonplaces—neglected or marginal sites and commonplace materials or things. It allows others to see landscape through a new lens, a lens less enamored with ideal and unattainable nature and more accepting of the real landscape in all its nitty-grittyness. But, as Schwartz's commissions increasingly include the permanent and the public, one wonders if it might not be possible to integrate artistic expression, cultural critique, rhetorical gesture with the making of place and the creation of a masterpiece. Masterpieces have come to mean beautiful compositions commissioned by wealthy patrons, made of enduring materials, but unfortunately devoid of content or meaning. Can a practice devoted to transfiguring the commonplace while building in public view and in marginal places aspire to the creation of masterpieces?

Martha Schwartz has 15 years of experiments, temporary installations, small commissions, and loyal patrons behind her. A review of this body of work as a whole reveals the power of a cultural critique more substantial than the rhetorical gestures of individual projects. Rendered sculpturally and spatially in plastic, pressed concrete, and mass-produced parts, this design practice-as-cultural critique has offered the profession a way to construct a world in the tough, sprawling commercial landscape of the strip, the highway, and suburb. If there is a territory in the late 20th century that is in desperate need of place-making not predicated on ersatz traditional urbanism, it is the urban-suburban edge, the realm of parking lots, shopping malls, fast food and big-box retail corridors, and our home, the place most Americans live. Now that this common place and problem has been represented to us, transfigured from a nowhere to a somewhere, perhaps others will follow Martha Schwartz's lead. Rather than seeing her as an iconoclast, a one-liner, and a destroyer of the profession, this critic thinks it's time to acknowledge her substantial critical and constructed contributions to both the American landscape and landscape architecture. (Notes on page 160)

Acknowledgments

Over the past eight years, I have worked out many of my ideas about contemporary landscape architecture in the company of my students, first at Harvard University and now at the University of Virginia. I owe them thanks for providing me with an ever enthusiastic and discerning audience. In addition, student research and writing for my class has altered or clarified my understanding of specific designers. In particular, Sigrid Cook, Kevin Rasmussen, Alison Ingram, and Eric Chou have deepened my appreciation of Martha Schwartz's designs for Rio Shopping Center, the Splice Garden, and CIT. Finally, I would like to thank Kaki Martin of Martha Schwartz's office for assisting me by providing verbal and graphic descriptions of the firm's work.

Gardens

Stella's Garden

Necco Garden

Whitehead Institute
Splice Garden

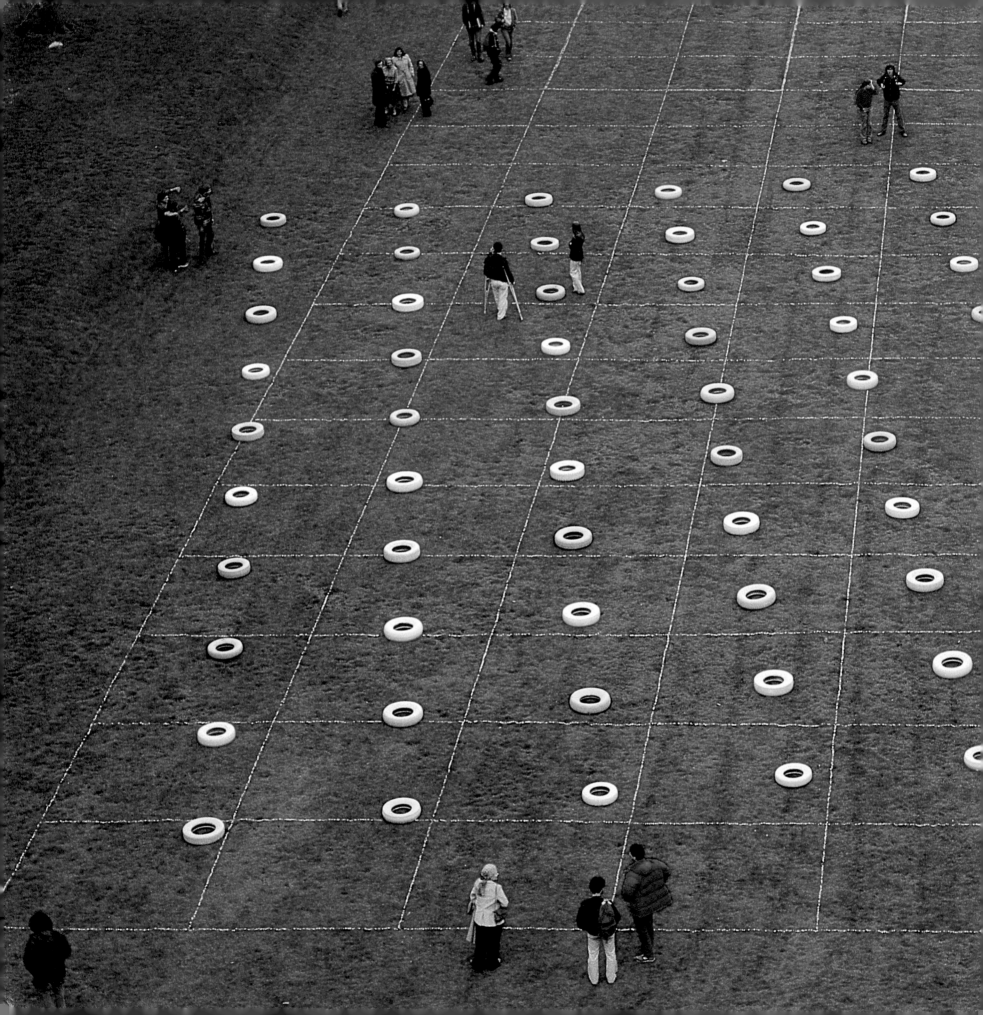

King County Jailhouse Garden

Center for Innovative
Technology

Rio Shopping Center

International Swimming
Hall of Fame

Limed Parterre with Skywriter

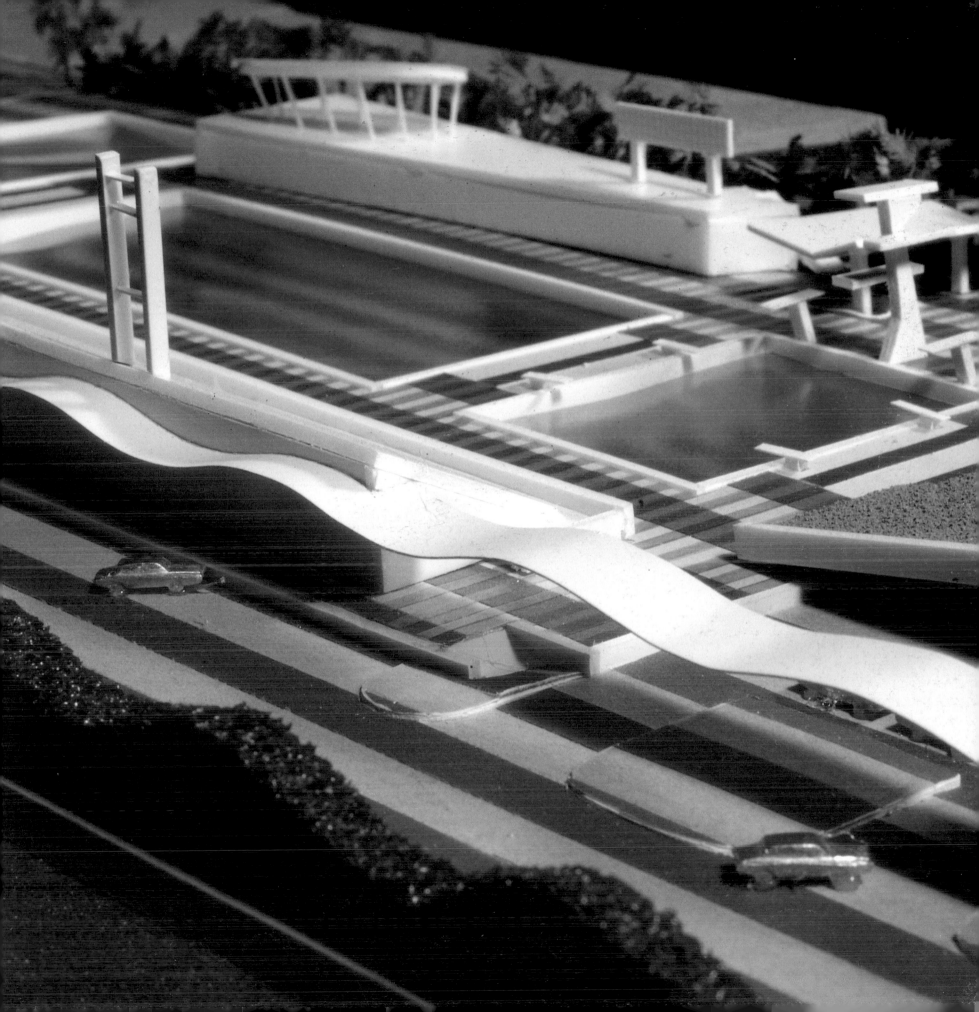

New England Holocaust
Memorial Competition

Kunsthal Museumpark
Competition

Biosphere Competition

Los Angeles Center

Columbia Center

Moscone Center Competition

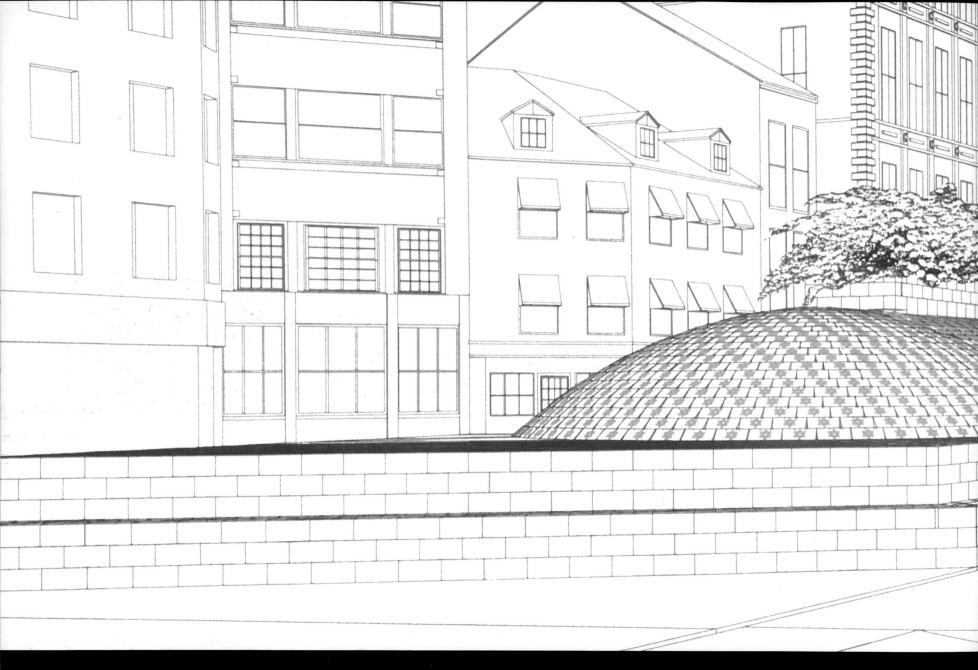

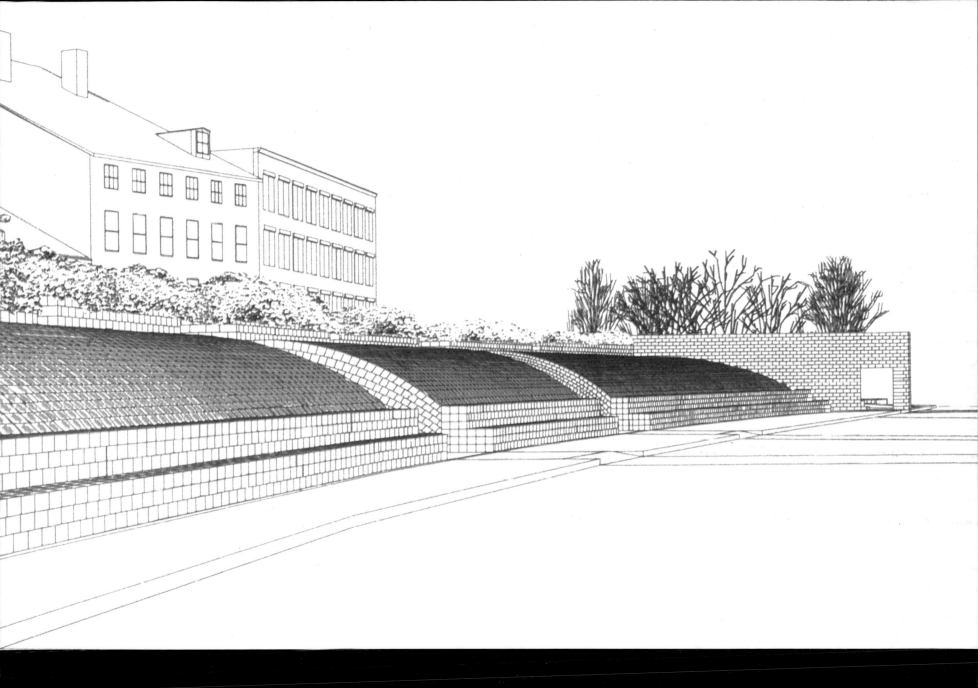

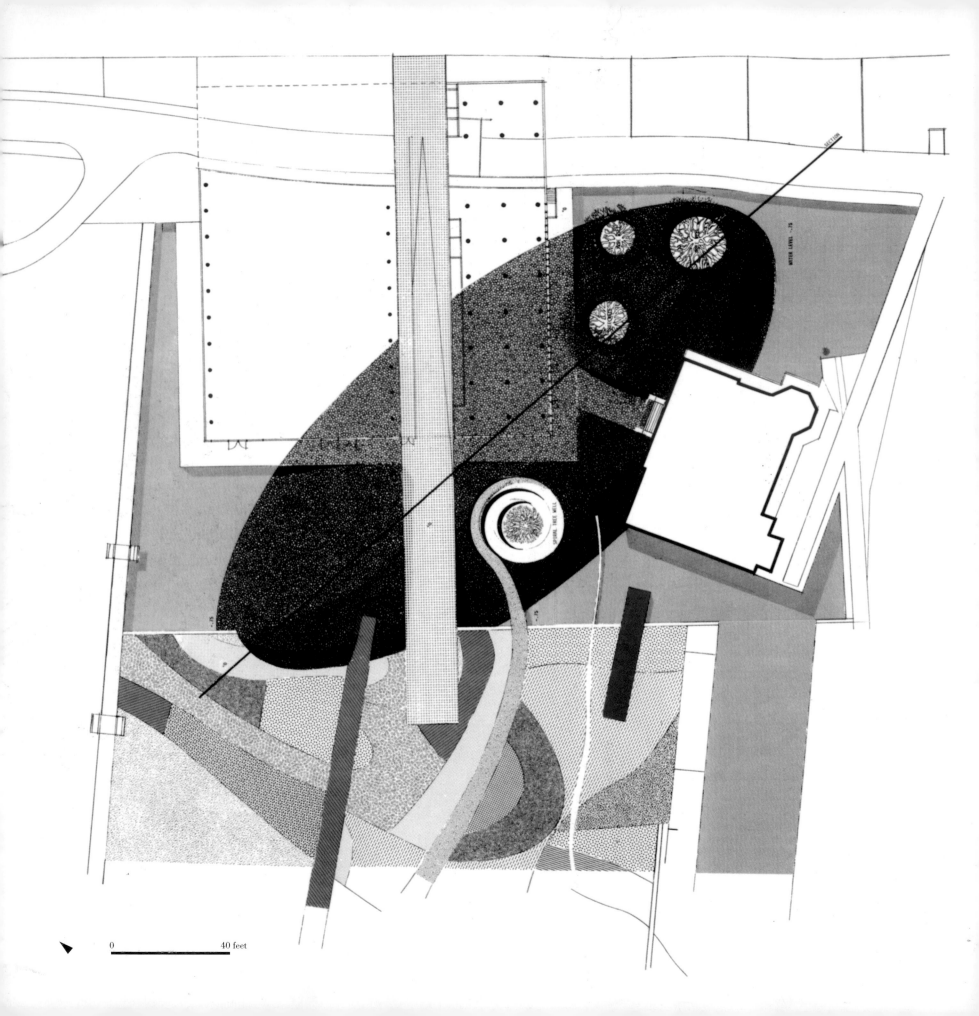

SPIRAL TREE WELL

WATER LEVEL ...75

SECTION

0   40 feet

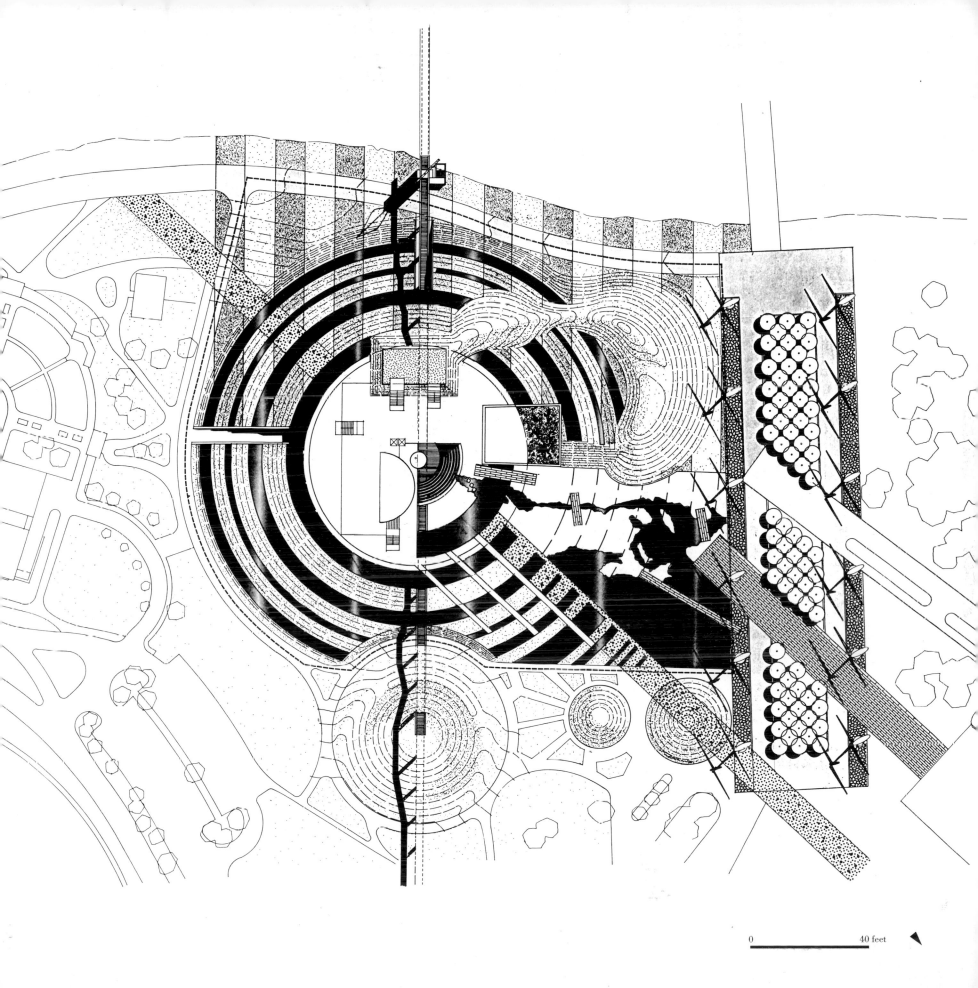

0 ————————— 40 feet

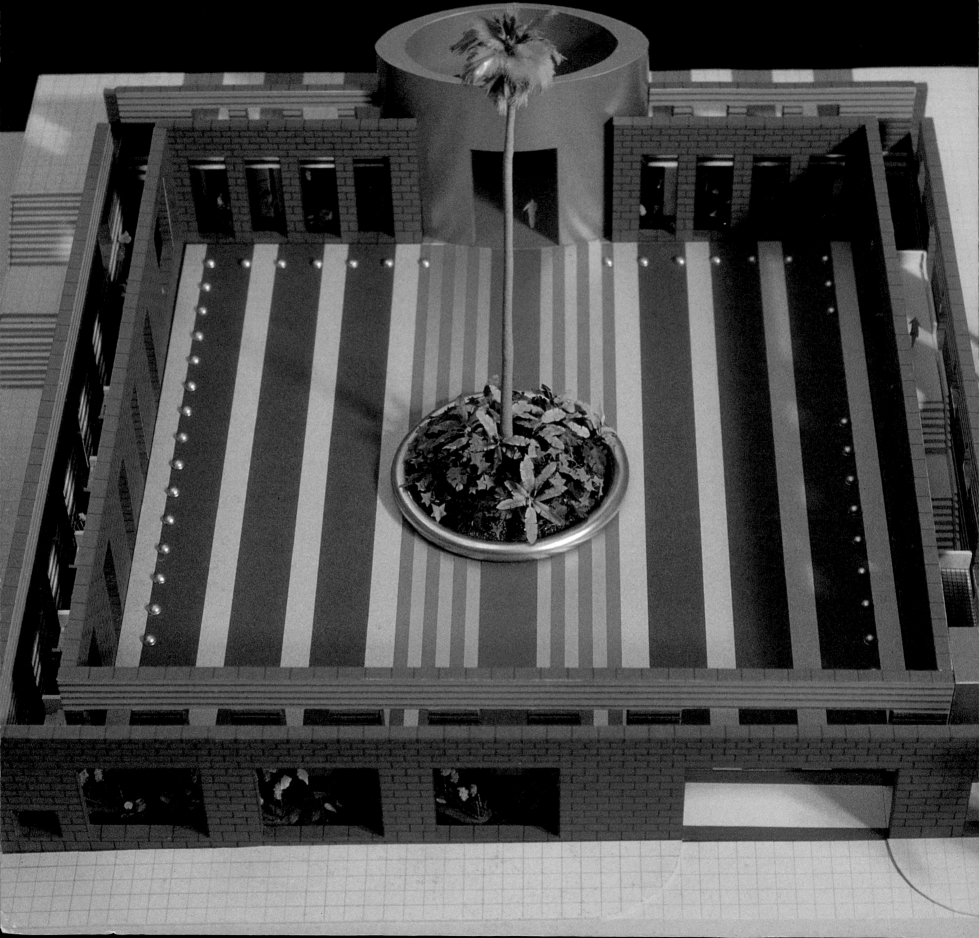

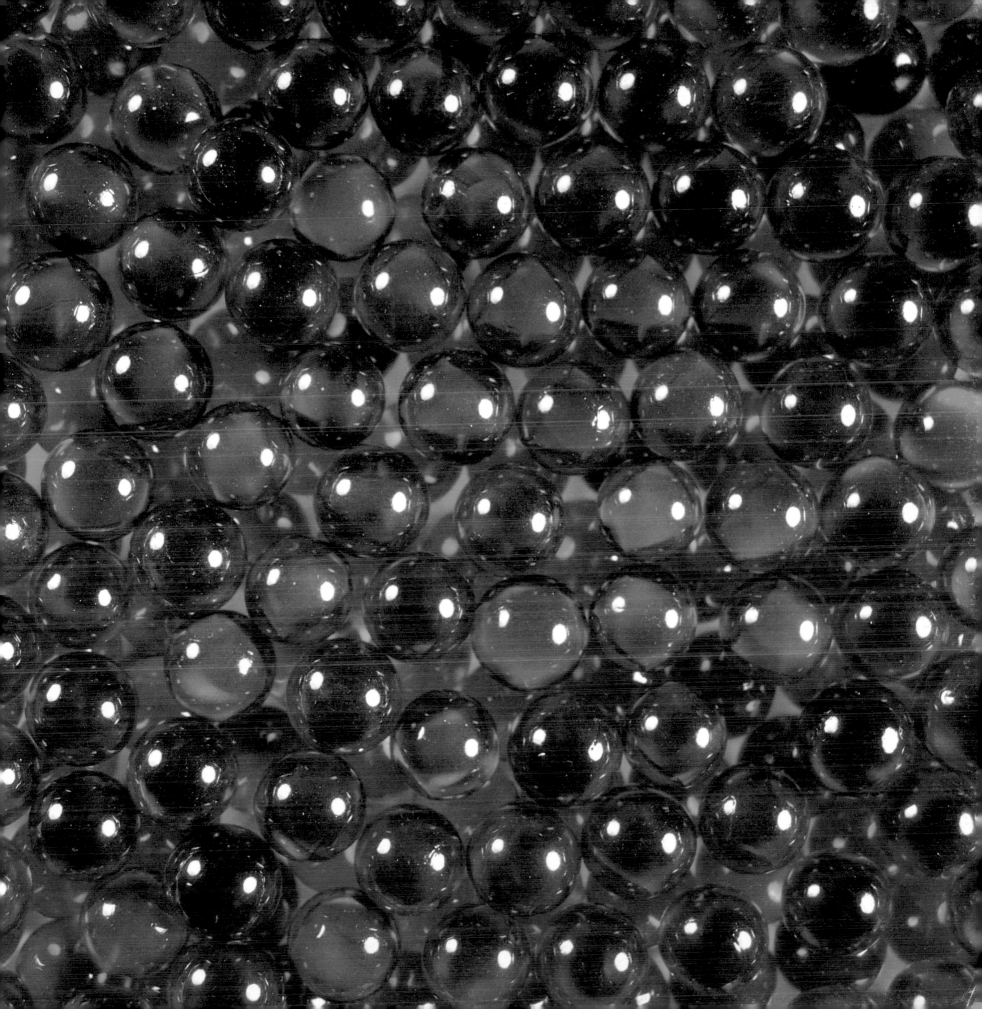

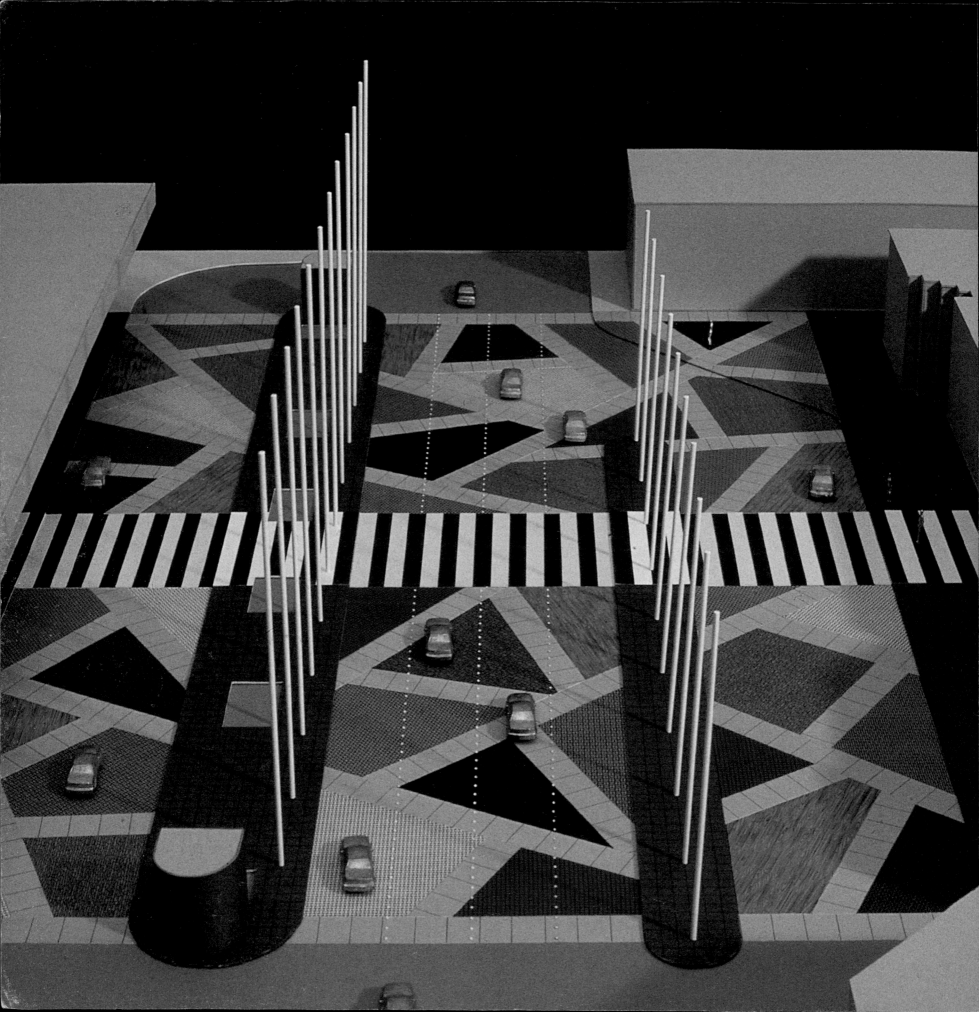

Fukuoka International Housing

Dickenson Residence

73

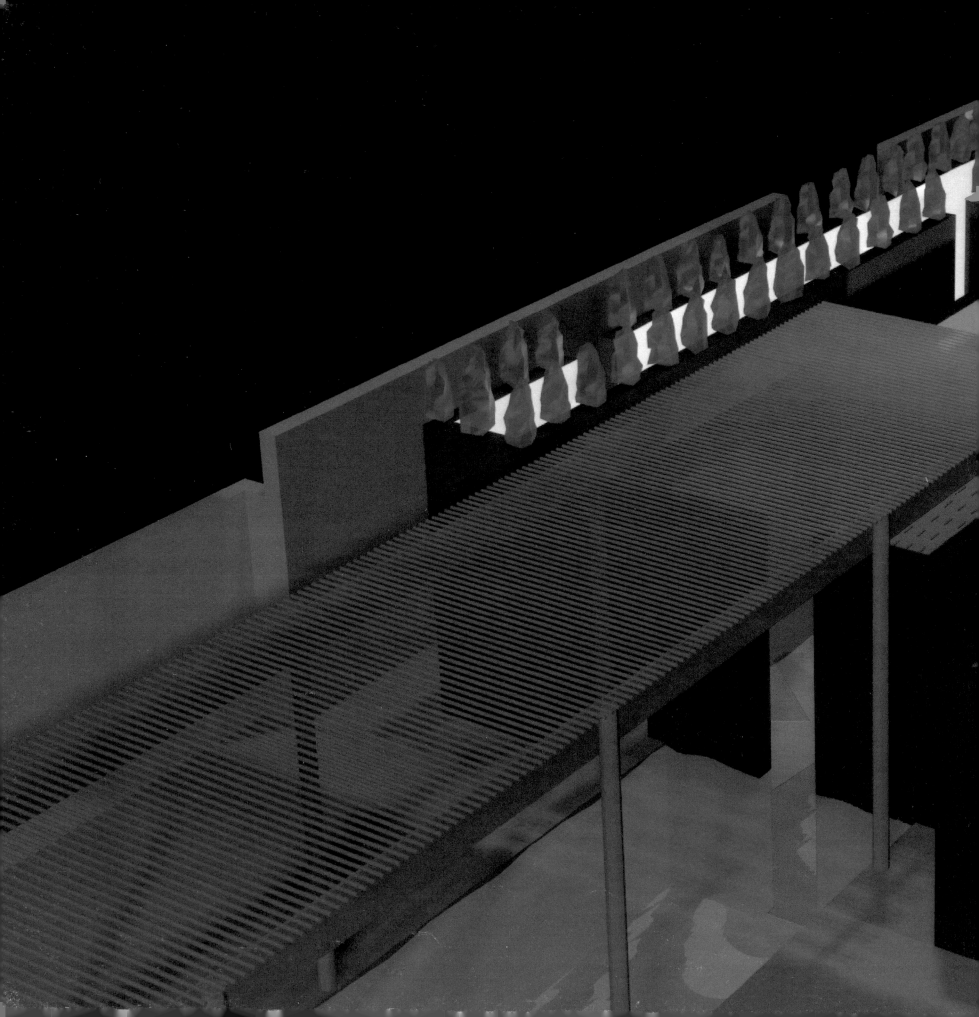

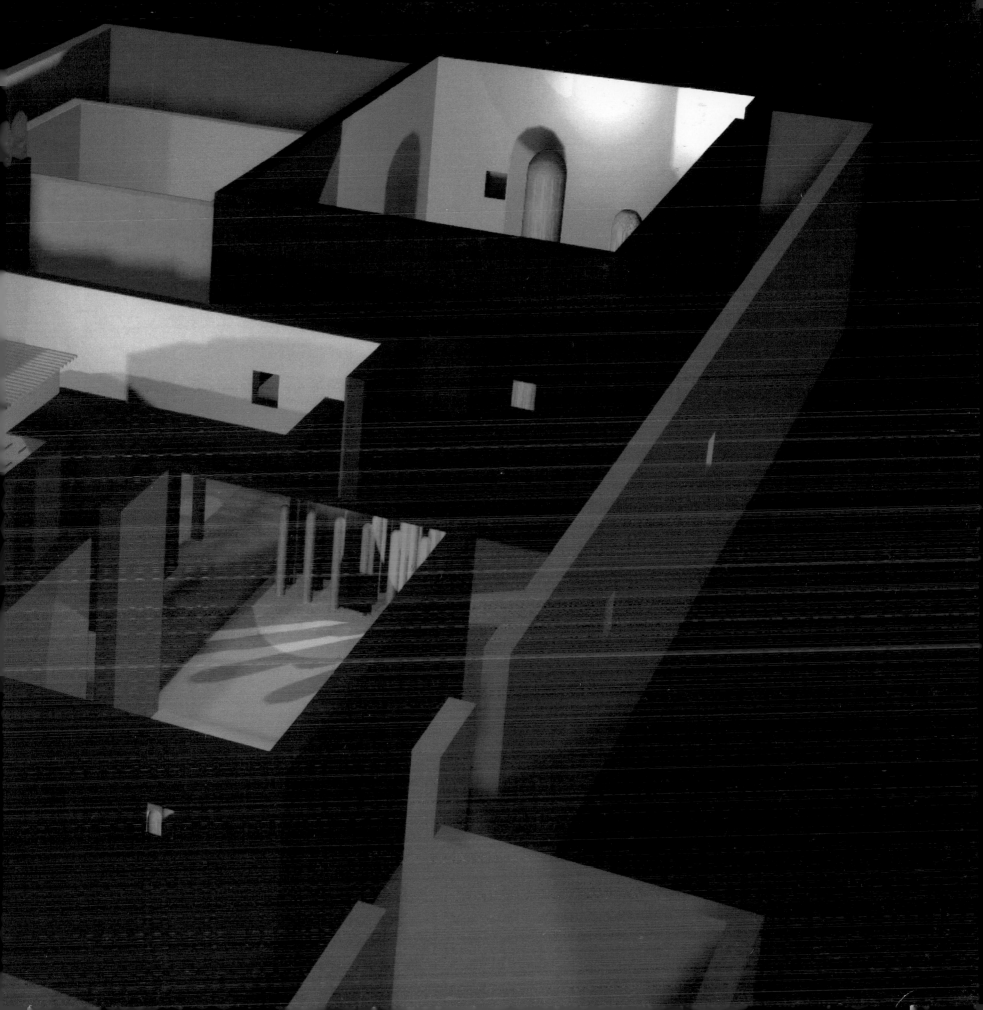

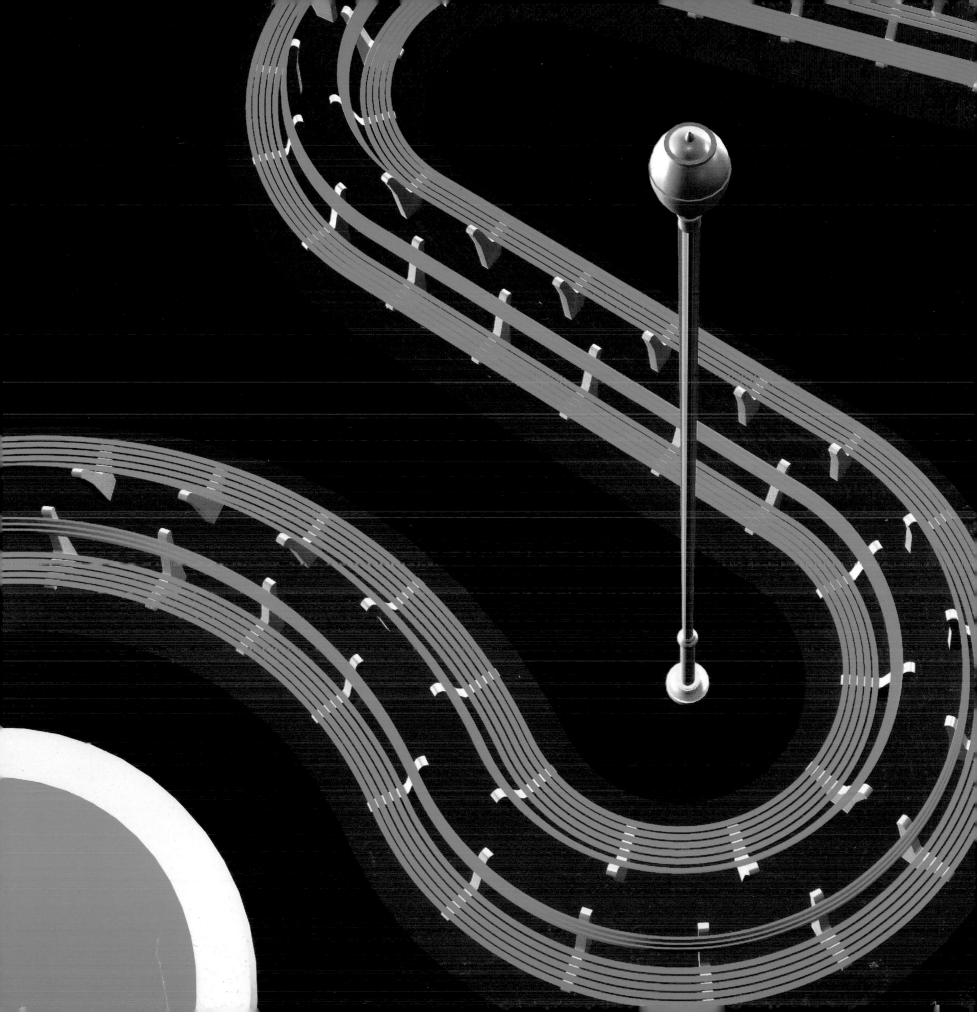

World Cup 1994

The Littman Wedding

Federal Courthouse Plaza

Baltimore Inner Harbor
Competition

Landschaftspark München - Riem

Miami International
Airport Sound Wall

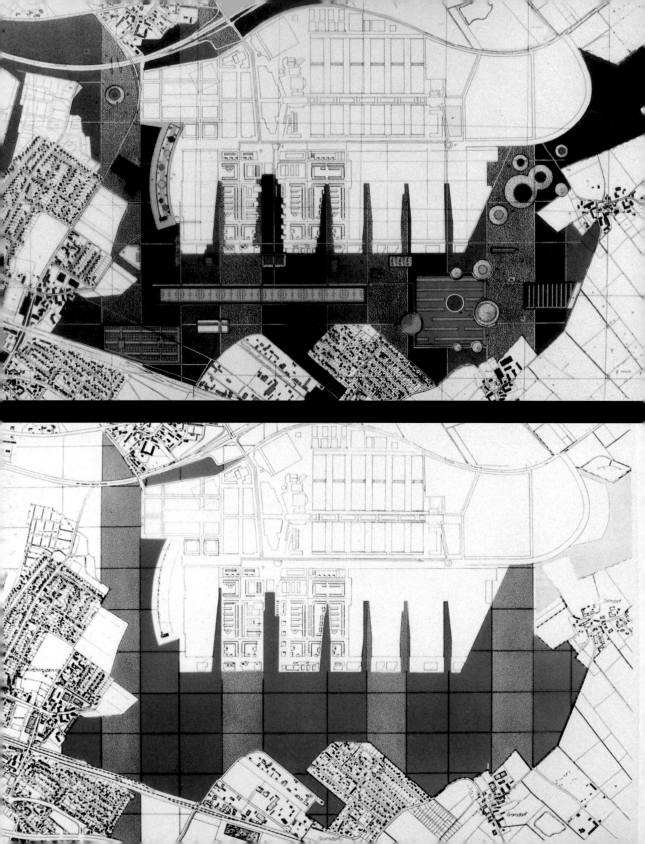

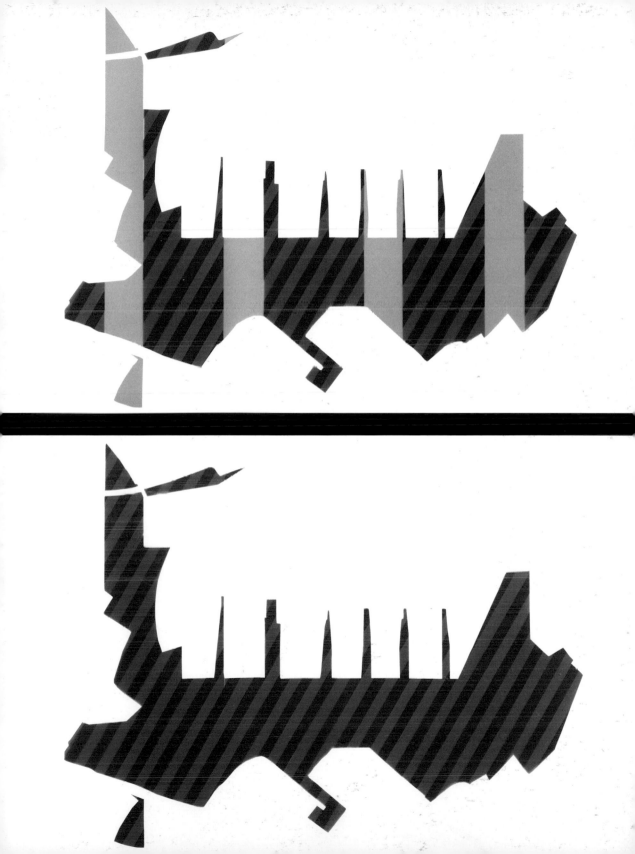

Interview with

Martha Schwartz

Known for arranging off-the-shelf or temporary materials, Day-Glo colors, and geometric patterns in unconventional designs, Martha Schwartz has occasionally shocked a profession steeped in the legacy of Frederick Law Olmsted. Schwartz has nevertheless designed landscapes that appear to be more challenging, wry, and innovative with each commission. Here, she talks about the influences that guide her work for private, corporate, and public clients.

You're known for incorporating unusual materials in the landscape. Could you discuss your choice of materials?

At first, my materials stemmed from my interest in Pop Art. I was drawn to the subversive quality of using lowly materials and discarded objects. I was attracted to artwork such as Jasper Johns' light bulb made of bronze—that unlikely expression of the commonplace with the precious. The elevation of everyday objects was an anti-mainstream art notion that intrigued me. I loved Andy Warhol's Brillo boxes, and his challenge to the art world as to what was considered to be "Art." At that time, most people thought that Brillo boxes clearly did not belong in museums. I believed that rules within the art establishment could and should be broken. The earthworks artists interested me for the same reasons: their work was conceptual and site specific; it couldn't be coopted by the gallery world. I wanted to challenge conventional thought and beliefs long before I ever knew landscape architecture existed.

When I started studying landscape architecture, I realized the profession invests a great deal in the lore of craftsmanship, tradition, and the use of high-quality materials. I thought there was entirely too much value placed on craft and materials, and a lack of concern or interest in the conceptual aspects of a work. In art, the concept is central to the work; in landscape, function is central.

I thought the lack of rigor toward concepts and ideas was perhaps tied to the focus on materials and craftsmanship. Maybe landscape architecture could move forward if we were encouraged to think of materials in a more expansive way. We could increase our conceptual language; granite curbs could be reconstituted plastic, glass, marbles, or Astroturf. In language, one's lack of vocabulary limits what one can think. In the same way, the lack of material possibilities limited conceptual thinking in landscape architecture.

Elevation of materials associated with low culture was my stance at the time. Now, however, I'm the queen of low-budget jobs. I've never done a project where I've been able to specify cut stone. My designs are made out of inexpensive materials because my clients cannot afford to build expensive projects. I have made a niche for myself by saying, "Okay, so you can't spend $40 a square foot—we'll do something with integrity and merit for $7. We'll use poured-in-place concrete or asphalt, and we'll approach it as a positive thing."

How do clients respond when you propose these inexpensive materials?

The changing reality is that we have fewer resources. Being able to make something remarkable out of humble materials is no longer a choice, it's a necessity. People believe we artists and designers have choices in selecting the level of materials; in reality, it is the client who sets the stage by establishing a budget. When a project is being established, I'm not there to ask, "How much do you *really* value this landscape? Does it have to last for 100 years, or only for an afternoon?" Those values are reflected by how much money goes into a project—a very easy measuring stick. I can try to persuade people to change those values, but budgets are not something I establish. I react to them.

In general, in this country, we don't value landscape or public space. The use of cheap materials is a reflection of that. I try to put some spirit into a place that is usually devalued or undervalued, and to imbue the landscape with some magic or meaning that transcends the fact that its owner only wants to spend $7 a square foot. That's less than what you spend on a carpet.

Trying to find virtue in lowly, inexpensive materials is inevitable if one wishes to proceed into the future with optimism. The world isn't going to revert back to centralized wealth or to the craftsman tradition. We're not going to go back to carving stone. The demise of craft is part of democratization, of spreading the wealth around. We live in a time when everyone will have to make do with smaller pieces of the pie.

Many of the choices we make in terms of materials reflect a level of cultural dishonesty. I encounter it often. Clients are often uncomfortable with low-quality materials, but they are also unwilling or unable to add money to the budget in order to meet their own standards. This leads to what I call the "veneer problem." A client may tell you they want the "look" of, for instance, granite, which means they want people to perceive something that doesn't exist. The objective, in which I as the designer am expected to collude, is to design an environment that creates an impression that the project is more valuable than it is. As long as stamped concrete will give the "look" of stone, the objective has been met.

I find that terribly dishonest. I'm not in the business of trying to fake people out. If you can only afford pressed concrete, then the question is, how can you apply that pressed concrete in support of an idea? It should be a means of expression, not a tool to fool somebody, or to present a facade for somebody's own conceit about who they would like to be, or who they want others to think they are. I believe that any design or art work of importance has integrity.

Art is often an exploration of that which is essential, pure, or elemental—the communication of a mood, feeling, or idea is necessary if art is to impact culture. The more direct and honest one can be in an expression, the more direct the communication. Plastic doesn't bother me at all unless one is trying to make someone think it's leather. Intellectual dishonesty and pretentiousness indicate that people are uncomfortable with who they are. When a designer tries to fool other people by creating a veneer, it brings us farther away from understanding who we are.

What is your response to critics who complain that you're not a landscape architect because you don't like plants?

I use plants when the situation calls for them. Again, many people don't understand the amount of commitment it takes to make a landscape, especially in an urban situation. In order to create a landscape on a garage top or a deck, you have to introduce more steel to support its weight; such construction is very expensive. And then you have to take care of it. Having a landscape is like deciding to have a child or a pet: If you don't have enough money to build or care for the project properly, then you shouldn't have it. If there are no plants in our projects, it usually means there is no budget or ability to maintain them.

You work with a bright color palette. Could you talk about the way you incorporate color in your landscape designs?

I've always loved bright colors, ever since I was a little girl. It's like liking candy. One of my grandmothers had a childlike delight of color. She brought me back gaudy *tchotchkes* from Florida, and she had plaster ducks and plastic flowers in her yard all year. When everyone else's yard was gray and snowy, she would have patches of beautifully colored flowers. As a little girl, I didn't critically judge her garden as unnatural, or lacking good taste—we're talking about dreary northeast Philadelphia here. I took as much delight in those colors as she did.

I've always loved looking at colors. I have not allowed myself to outgrow that delight. It's important to protect some of the childlike qualities within oneself. It still excites me to see bright colors, and they look even more powerful outside.

As we grow up, we learn what is tasteful and acceptable to others. We learn not to be excited by loud, bright colors, glitter, the visual palette we are introduced to as a growing child. The whole issue of tastefulness is repellant to me. "Taste" is a set of dictated rules about how one should look, act, and feel. Our culture is phobic about color as well. The lack of color in our culture is a northern European holdover. When people see bright color, they're often delighted or relieved. It signals to them that they are allowed to be more free in how they act. It's amazing how powerful a signal color can be, and how directly it can convey a mood.

Who are the landscape architects whose work you admire?

Perhaps my most important inspiration has come from the work of Isamu Noguchi. When I began to study landscapes, I was very influenced by his horizontal sculptures about earth forming, and his stage sets for Martha Graham. Noguchi transcended the lines between art, design, and landscape. His landscapes create magical, surreal places.

You've written that the art of landscape architecture is to define the relationship between nature and culture. Can you elaborate?

I want to use the landscape to speak about being human, to communicate ideas. The landscapes I find most wonderful are those that recognize something about our humanness and reflect it back to us. Looking at a great landscape is like looking at a mirror or a portrait.

Many people hear the term "landscape" and think that it means "nature." Natural landscapes play an important role in our culture. But what interests me most is the landscape we make and occupy. In my work, the question I'm always asking is, "How does the landscape reflect who we are and who we want to be?"

I've always loved manipulating living materials to our needs. I'm fascinated with the use of outdoor spaces as "rooms" we can inhabit. I am intrigued by landscapes in which trees are manipulated to make hallways, where vines are made into shelters, and hedges are made to form rooms. I'm most thrilled by these transitional places that are neither nature nor architecture.

I grew up in Philadelphia. We used to go to Longwood Gardens to visit incredible greenhouses that contained formal gardens with floors made of grass. I would fantasize about living in a house where you could get up in the morning and your feet would first touch a carpet of living grass. I don't believe that transforming nature to meet our needs is automatically destructive if one considers humans as part of nature. I believe one can and should form cities, houses, and rooms—places to eat and relax, places to live—out of landscape.

Your love of nature is for nature controlled. How do feel about, for example, Yosemite?

To me, the beauty of ideas is as meaningful as the beauty of nature. I am energized by the power and beauty of ideas. I love cities: they are the repositories of culture. I am more excited by what I can see and hear in New York than by what I could see and hear in Yosemite.

107

But I would never say wilderness is unimportant. I think it is important in an abstract way. We all need to know that the wilderness exists—that if we had to get to it, we could. But very few of us now experience actual wilderness—it's an abstract notion to most Americans. To get to the wilderness, you have to make a big effort; you get in a plane, then you get in a car. You're there briefly, and then you leave. I'm not sure we couldn't be happy with virtual wilderness—on a computer screen, or in a virtual reality mode. Being in the wilderness is a far more abstract experience than living in a city or a suburb. The wilderness is a romantic fantasy that we carry with us, but it's not part of our reality.

Unfortunately, much of the resistance to landscape architecture has to do with Americans' wilderness fantasy. While imagining that we inhabit a beautiful wilderness, we have allowed an incredible amount of ugliness to spread across the landscape. We are so blinded by our wilderness fantasy that anything that is *not* wilderness is left untended or forgotten. Since a shopping center isn't wilderness, its landscape doesn't deserve any special treatment. It's okay to surround it with a parking lot with no trees.

The idea that a shopping center parking lot could become a viable, interesting landscape capable of modifying the environment is an idea Americans have not discovered. We won't spend the money, make the laws, or spend the time and effort to make it possible for landscape and parking to be designed together.

You've written that we treat the landscape the way Victorians regarded women—as either virgins or whores.

That's right. People compartmentalize the landscape in their minds. Landscape is mainly thought of as a pure remnant of nature. "Landscape" exists in parks and in Yosemite. The idea that landscapes exist as a parking lot, a rooftop, or a median strip is hard for people to imagine. "Nature" involves picturesque visions; if it isn't picturesque, or natural, then we allow our landscapes to be indiscriminately degraded. We haven't really come up with a name for the landscapes we have created for ourselves to live in.

Are other cultures better at shaping public landscape?

The cultures of France, Germany, Holland, Spain, Japan, and Italy are much better. Our failure is perhaps the most disappointing because we are so wealthy and capable. A lot of countries are so hungry for development that their disregard for landscape, though deplorable, is understandable. It's hard to convince people to build in an ecologically responsible or beautiful way when they need development, jobs, commerce.

We, on the other hand, ought to be more forward-thinking in valuing our landscape. We have the means to create environments that respond to the way we live. I mean "environments" to include our urban, suburban, and agricultural landscapes. Places like France and Holland are much more advanced in thinking about landscape as outdoor spaces that include and respond to human use.

And what do landscape artists and designers in these countries do differently?

Holland is producing some of the most sophisticated landscape architects in the world today. The Dutch have a head start because they have manufactured their landscape from the very beginning—the land they occupy they created from the ocean. They have no fantasy of the untouched, unspoiled wilderness. They are freer to think about how to manipulate the landscape because they've constructed it from the beginning.

In most European countries, the environments where people live—highways, railroads, and city streets—are much more beautiful than ours. These countries support their artists and designers, which proves the value the culture has for the quality of the visual environment. The French, for example, identify with their built landscape and see themselves through it. We, however, do not. We view art and design as an adjunct treatment—the cherry on the cake. Americans don't perceive the strip shopping centers on the outskirts of all our cities as symbols of our national identity. We don't identify with the land in that way. We identify with the fantasy images of picturesque landscapes on billboards, in magazine ads, or on TV, but never with the places where we live.

Our highways, bridges, roads, parks, and infrastructure are viewed as environments that are utilitarian, where there is no need or room for art. Every time I get off the plane after travelling in other countries, I see what a narrow view we have of what is essential to life. Functionality as a value reigns over beauty. We're a nation of low riders; we don't really value beauty, and it shows.

How do you propose to create a climate where valuing the built landscape is acceptable? How can we learn to value parking lots, strip malls, and medians?

I'm not an evangelist. However, I teach and hope that what I build will make the landscape visible to those who usually don't see it. Perhaps I can open it up as an area of opportunity to those who might want to explore the landscape as designers or artists. I often feel as if I'm simply reacting to the marketplace, but I usually end up educating the client to the possibilities inherent in the landscape, project by project. It's a slow process.

It's very difficult to teach someone about the value of art and design if they have had no previous training or exposure to them. Many of my clients are very smart and well-educated in most areas. But they often don't have a basis for understanding visual ideas. They simply don't have information about the the topic of art. In this country, art and art history are no longer taught in schools. If you aren't exposed to aesthetic ideas at home, there is little chance of educating yourself through the culture. Other cultures embrace a more integrated approach to aesthetics. The general lack of understanding and support for what we do in the United States poses a dilemma for many landscape architects, artists, and architects. Do we get on a plane and go to Japan, because the Japanese value the role of aesthetics in the environment? Or should we try to bolster interest and support here? If we choose to focus our work in the USA, how do we proceed in an era of dwindling resources?

In one of your lectures, you tell the audience that you are looking for corporations and institutions that will embrace this idea of bettering the built environment. Have you found any?
I have done some public work now for the General Services Administration (GSA). But even in public work, you need one person willing to take a risk and stand by you. Unfortunately, most people who work in the public realm are risk averse. People vote for them, they come up for review, they aren't autonomous. So it's a much more difficult task to find someone who will stand by you through the entire process. You need someone committed to the belief that you as an artist or designer have something important to contribute to the public realm.

We are on the brink of completing a number of government projects—Jacob Javits Plaza in Manhattan, the HUD plaza in Washington, D.C., and a plaza for the new federal courthouse being built in Minneapolis. These projects are a tremendous opportunity. Government projects are known for being bland and noncontroversial, founded on a belief that public projects must meet every user's criteria. This always results in a design that has been reduced to the lowest common denominator to avoid political problems. For me, these projects are an experiment in whether it is possible to do interesting and adventuresome public work. None of these projects is expensive. Everything has to go through reviews. We have an enlightened patron within the GSA who is there to make sure that the wings don't get torn off the butterfly, to make sure the artistic intent remains an important component.

Is there anything the GSA projects have in common?
These plazas—Javits, HUD, Minneapolis—are typical of plazas constructed around buildings in the 1960s. According to the modernist tenets of that time, buildings stood in space as heroic sculptural objects set upon the empty, utopian ground plane. Architects typically eliminated everything near the building to avoid competition with its sculptural form. Empty plazas set atop parking lots produced dead spaces at the bottoms of buildings. Over the years, people have tried to inhabit these places but with no great success.

Many of our major downtowns were built in the expansionist era of the 1960s, when these blank plazas were constructed. Post-modernism offered a critique of these spaces. We decided that maybe the street wall is good after all, that big blank plazas create voids, and that we should create more humane environments at the bottoms of buildings. The primacy of buildings as sculpture was questioned. There has been a reassessment, and an attempt to retrofit and reinhabit these spaces.

These three GSA projects all convey a wry, lighthearted mood. What is the role of humor in your designs?
My whole family has a great sense of humor. It may stem from Jewish tradition—humor is a powerful tool that allows people to face issues too painful to confront. The old adage that comedy is a very serious business is absolutely true. Most great comedy stems from anger; I have observed that comedians are often the angriest people. I, too, am a fairly angry person. I seem to run on anger. Humor is a socially acceptable method of giving vent to anger and frustration. Humor opens people up—they're more receptive. They are delighted when they are made to laugh at something—it's relief.

Discuss your design for Jacob Javits Plaza, the former site of Richard Serra's "Tilted Arc."
Our version of Javits Plaza is a reaction to the "Tilted Arc" sculpture. I wanted it to be the antithesis of the "Tilted Arc"—less self-important and self-referential. It's simpler in its ambitions: just an accommodating place to sit down and have lunch. The "Tilted Arc" was a critique of modernist architecture, and an expression of alienation. It was a powerful confrontation. In our Javits Plaza, you don't have to engage in confrontation. You can just have lunch.

The public art world learned a great deal through the trials of the "Tilted Arc." The use of the plaza was subverted for the artist's vision, and whether that subversion is appropriate for public art turned out to be a very valuable discussion. I changed my mind during that sequence of events about what public art should be. It has to function on more than one level. It's not in a gallery. People don't have a choice of whether to deal with it. The best public art is art that can speak on many levels, and if you choose not to be engaged with it, you don't have to be.

What advice would you give to civic officials trying to upgrade their urban spaces?
Most of our public spaces are ignored and abused, bland and poorly designed. No sense of place has been achieved, largely because no risks

have been taken. It takes courage to back a vision, but public projects are largely in the purview of public officials who are particularly vulnerable to scrutiny. If we want plazas, parks, streets, parking lots, and rooftops that people can claim as their own, it is imperative that city officials demand more from the designers of these spaces. We make demands of architects, but landscape architecture has not been viewed as an art form. It is important that public officials set higher standards and require that these spaces be characterized by personality and spirit. For landscape to be functional, it must be claimed by people, emotionally and spiritually.

Could you talk about the psychological costs to Americans of our degraded landscapes? You've said that healing our landscapes could help to heal our social pathologies.

I believe that the environments we live in absolutely go to the core of how we define ourselves and what our expectations are, what we hope for. People inherently react to something beautiful. It's not something you learn through slide shows. People respond to the quality of space, the proportion of space, color, light, rhythm, texture. It doesn't take much to imagine the psychological effect on someone of going from an urban tenement to a beautiful room full of light and air, or from a street of strip mall parking lots to the Champs-Elysées.

We tend to believe that people don't see or feel those differences, but they do. People live better in places that look and feel better. We aren't animals living out in the wilderness, we're human beings.

Art is a measure of health. If art flourishes in a culture, it means that the basic needs of living are met: finding shelter, not being at war, having a government that is stable, having food, having a certain amount of predictability. Once you've taken care of those things, what do you do? You dream, write, paint, make gardens. Garden-making is a true luxury, which is why there are so few cultures that have actually developed an indigenous garden vernacular. It takes a stable, wealthy culture to produce these environments. My frustration is that we as Americans could produce environments that are better for us, but we choose not to.

Can you talk about your use of geometry in the landscape?

Right angles and lines are human constructs. When we impose a geometric order on the landscape, we inhabit the landscape with human thought. Geometry clearly defines a man-made, rather than natural environment. If you wanted to have something read or be seen in the inherent chaos of nature, the quickest way is to bring geometric order into it. Geometry is also an extension of the city, a way of integrating the built work into an existing grid.

I'm interested in orchestrating one's experience through space. This is not easy to do outdoors because of the scale, which is much larger than architectural scale, and because of the chaotic nature of outdoor space. We carry geometric forms around like maps in our heads—we can remember what a circle or a square looks like. So if you impose such forms on the ground, it is a way of orienting people in space. Whereas if people engage an amoeboid or naturalistic form, with which they've had no previous experience, it is much more dislocating. You're never sure where you are. You need familiar mental maps in outdoor space.

For example, the Citadel is a very highly regularized landscape, a serial landscape in which familiar forms are repeated. That repetition produces a reference to architectural space, and defines a room. The room inside which something happens is a common theme in my work, as rooms are made for the purpose of human habitation. This in itself is a powerful contrast with nature.

What is your definition of a garden?

A garden, as opposed to a landscape, is a place that offers a sense of separation from the outside world. That separation must be created by making a threshold—whether real or implied. This threshold creates the ability to leave one world and enter another. That is the fundamental function of a garden: to allow a person the psychological space to dream, think, rest, or disengage from the world. It functions as an interruption of daily routine, like entering a church or a temple. It is meant to describe another type of psychological space, to help you touch your real self.

What is the prognosis for landscape architecture in America?

We have to redefine what we consider to be landscape. I think of landscape as anything outside the building footprint—the road, the highway, the parking lot, and everything in between. If we see it only as attendant to architecture—parks, gardens, and plazas—landscape architecture is going to become a much more marginalized profession. We have to concentrate on becoming more useful. We must engage the less sexy, less prestige-oriented projects and begin to deal with our physically and visually degraded landscape. That is our future. Designing gardens for wealthy people can be very rewarding, but it will not be enough to keep us vital as a profession.

Living in an environmentally balanced world is becoming increasingly important. However, there are many people who feel that design is not important to making landscape environmentally sound. I think those are false poles that are set up by the profession. My hope is that our sensitivity to our environment will one day include addressing the visual quality of all our built environments. That is going to be our role: to create sound and healthy environments that are also beautiful and meaningful places for human beings.

Garden Descriptions

Bagel Garden

Location: *Back Bay*
                Boston, MA
Date: *1979*
Photography: Alan Ward

Trained as an artist, Schwartz grew frustrated working as an apprentice in a Cambridge landscape architectural office. Longing for a speedy, inexpensive installation she could accomplish with her own hands, she tackled the 22-foot-square front garden of her own Georgian rowhouse in the Back Bay. Incorporating two concentric square hedges of an existing formal garden, Schwartz based her scheme upon French renaissance gardens that were designed as stage sets for dances and celebrations. Conceived as the stage set for her husband's return from a week-long business trip, the front yard also became an ode to the landscape artist's favorite food: "Bagels are humble, homey, and ethnic," she explains. "Besides, I could get many of them inexpensively."

Between the outer and inner squares of the 16-inch-high boxwood hedges Schwartz arranged a 30-inch-wide strip of purple aquarium gravel, dominated by a grid of eight dozen bagels, each dipped in marine spar for weatherproofing. Inside the inner square of hedge she planted 30 purple *Ageratum* to match the gravel and complement an existing Japanese maple. "Despite the many garden party guests who were helping celebrate the installation and my husband's return," Schwartz recalls, "he was not particularly amused." The family left within days for a summer in Europe; cats discovered the garden; the bagels eventually decomposed.

Formal arrangement of bagels seen through garden gate.

Bagel parterre in plan.

Stella's Garden

Location: *Bala - Cynwyd, PA*
Client: *Stella Schwartz*
Date: *1982*
Photography: *Martha Schwartz*

The garden Martha Schwartz created for her mother's duplex in suburban Philadelphia had to be indestructible: "My mother has a notoriously black thumb and has never had any luck with plants," Schwartz relates. It also had to be inexpensive, for it was built when Schwartz was trying out ideas in the landscape but had few clients of her own. The site was a dreary, untended 20-by-20-foot plot bordered by her mother's garage wall and the neighbor's mirror-image back yard. Mrs. Schwartz, a busy real estate saleswoman, demanded that the garden be easy to maintain. She never went into her garden, but viewed it from her kitchen and bedroom windows.

Schwartz's strategy was to transform the bleak, untended garden into a fantasy environment for viewing, much as one can gaze into a Fabergé egg. She collected junk from her mother's garage: chicken wire, rickety wooden ladders, abandoned garbage cans. Over the course of several months, she bought Plexiglas scraps by the pound. Since a spare, minimalist esthetic was in vogue at the time, she wanted to explore the idea of adding onto, rather than reducing, a scheme to its purest form.

A colored Plexiglas fence separates Stella's garden from its duplex counterpart. A patio, surfaced in aquarium gravel, supports a 10-by-10-foot platform for a cinderblock and wire-glass table. Two painted poles support a chicken-wire "cloud," or garden gate. Five trash cans along the driveway are painted with glitter and epoxy.

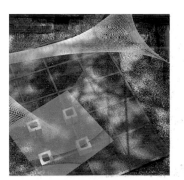

Plan view of wire-glass table and flying netting.

View from bedroom window through chicken-wire cloud.

Necco Garden

Location: Killian Court
           Massachusetts Institute of
           Technology
           Cambridge, MA
Client: Hayden Gallery, MIT
Date: May 1, 1980
Team: Martha Schwartz, Inc.
           Peter Walker
           Rebecca Schwartz
Photography: Alan Ward
             Martha Schwartz

Classic French gardens organize large spaces through the application of patterned horizontal planes, series of objects, and parallel lines that exaggerate distances. The Necco Garden, designed as a temporary (one-day) installation for the Massachusetts Institute of Technology's Hayden Gallery, echoes the principles and geometry of French gardens to reflect the grandeur and formality of the great court at MIT. Schwartz chose Necco wafers, the familiar pastel candy disks, because a Necco factory lies adjacent to the campus, providing a constant sweet aroma. (The company also donated 80,000 Neccos for the project.) Because the installation was constructed on May 1, the pastel colors of the Neccos are intended to evoke the joy that accompanies the first signs of spring.

An orthogonal grid of Necco wafers fills the 100-by-170-foot court and aligns with the surrounding architecture. A point grid of tires painted in colors that match the Neccos is rotated from the Necco grid to point toward a newly installed sculpture by Michael Heizer.

Through the imposition of a 10-by-10-foot grid drawn by lines of Neccos, the garden enlivens the ground plane of the great courtyard. The grid, aligned with the grid of Back Bay Boston across the Charles River, reflects MIT's larger urban context.

Aerial view of parterre and
Back Bay.

Close-up of parterre of Neccos
and tires.

Garage where tires were painted
to match Necco colors.

Arranging the Neccos.

Following string guidelines to
place Neccos.

Whitehead Institute
Splice Garden

Location: *Cambridge, MA*
Client: *Whitehead Institute*
                  for Biomedical Research
Date: *1986*
Team: *The Office of Peter Walker*
                  and Martha Schwartz
                  Bradley Burke
Execution: *Terry Lee Dill*
                  Robert Scheffman
Facilitator: *Aptikar Arts Management*
Photography: *Alan Ward*
                  Martha Schwartz

This 25-by-35-foot rooftop garden in Cambridge, Massachusetts is part of an adventuresome art collection assembled by Director David Baltimore for the Whitehead Institute, a microbiology research center.

The site was a lifeless rooftop courtyard atop a nine-story office building. Its dreary, tiled surface and high surrounding walls conspired to create a dark, inhospitable space, overlooked by both a classroom and a faculty lounge. The lounge offered access to the courtyard, making it a potential place to eat lunch.

Along with its spatial woes, the floor of the courtyard was constructed with a concrete decking system that could not hold weight. There also was no source of water for the rooftop, no maintenance staff, and a low budget, precluding the possibility of introducing living plants.

However, it was entirely possible to convey a sense of a planted garden by providing enough signals for the site to be read as a garden. "There are many examples of other cultures that create garden abstractions," notes Schwartz. "For example, in Japanese gardens, symbolic landscapes often imply a larger landscape. This was the strategy at Whitehead—to create a garden through abstraction, symbolism, and reference."

Schwartz wanted the narrative of the garden to relate to the work carried out by the Institute. The garden became a cautionary tale about the dangers inherent in gene splicing: the possibility of creating a monster.

This garden is a monster—the joining together like Siamese twins of gardens from different cultures. One side is based on a French renaissance garden, the other on a Japanese Zen garden. The elements that compose these gardens have been distorted: the rocks typically found in a

Zen garden are composed of topiary pompoms from the French garden. Other plants, such as palms and conifers, are in strange and unfamiliar associations. Some plants project off the vertical surface of the wall; others teeter precariously on the wall's top edge.

All the plants in the garden are plastic. The clipped hedges, which double as seating, are rolled steel covered in Astroturf. Green gravel and paint offer the strongest cues that this is a garden.

The intent was to create for the scientists who occupy this building a visual puzzle that could not be solved. The garden is an ode to "better living through chemistry."

Garden as viewed from classroom.

Plan view of splice.

Ground view along splice.

"Zen" garden portion.

"Zen topiary" element.

"Zen" wall piece.

King County Jailhouse Garden

Location: *Seattle, Washington*
Client: *King County Arts Commission*
Date: *1987*
Team: *The Office of Peter Walker*
     and Martha Schwartz
     Ken Smith
     Martin Poirier
     Bradley Burke
Architect: *NBBJ*
Execution: *Larry Tate/*
     Fabrication Specialties
Photography: *Martha Schwartz*
     Art on File
     James K. Fanning

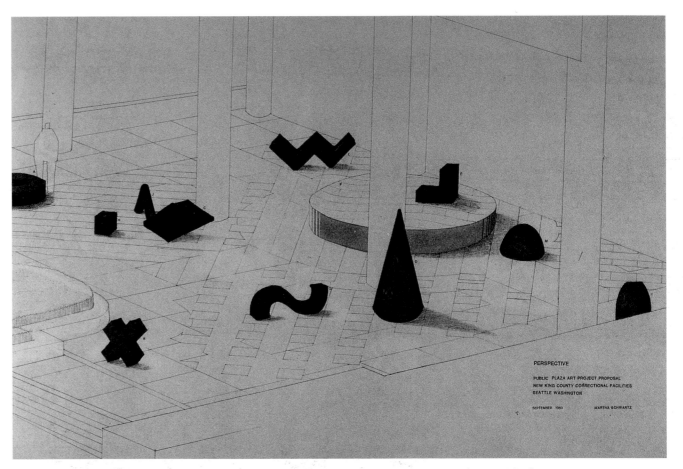

Axonometric view.

Seattle's new jail, designed without a lobby or a foyer, offered nowhere for attorneys, families with children, and other visitors to meet. A plaza garden of concrete and ceramic tile offers a lively, low maintenance meeting place. The plaza's surface is paved in fragments of broken tile. Sculptural forms, serving as children's play structures, echo hedges, topiary, parterres, and a fountain. Its surface is paved in broken tile alternating with stripes of exposed aggregate. A ceramic mural on the wall of the building behind the plaza suggests open space; the simple arch represents a garden gate, implying an exit. Although the image suggests the idea of escape, the tiled wall in fact imprisons.

The scheme is intended to focus attention on the ground plane and away from the overwhelming bulk of the building. The color and scale of the objects bring comfort to a harsh space; the "topiary" forms provide places to sit.

The tile fragments suggest that the garden is at its penultimate moment before disintegration. The colorful palette and subject matter belie a deeper message: a recognition of the chaos, danger, and fragility of prisoners' lives.

View from above reveals axis, cross-axis, circular "water element" and "topiary."

Circular "water element" and zigzag "fountain."

Topiary "tree-seat" and topiary hemispheres.

Topiary X warning sign at entry.

Close-up of hand-set broken tile at "water element."

Center for Innovative Technology

Location: *Fairfax, VA*
Client: *Center for Innovative Technology*
Date: *1988*
Team: *The Office of Peter Walker*
                and Martha Schwartz
                Ken Smith
                David Meyer
                Martin Poirier
Architect: *Arquitectonica International*
Photography: *Marc Treib*
                David Walker
                Peter Walker

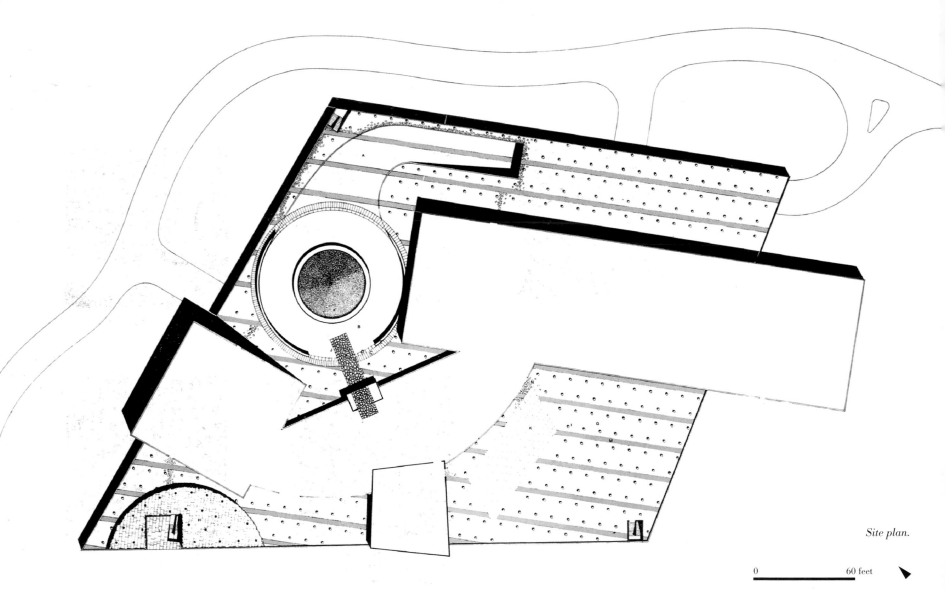

Site plan.

0 _____ 60 feet ▶

The Fairfax, Virginia-based Center for Innovative Technology, a government-backed entity that markets scientific research, provided Schwartz with her first opportunity to collaborate with the Miami-based architects Arquitectonica. The 43,000-square-foot site includes the top of a trapezoidal four-story parking garage on top of which sits a village of oddly shaped office buildings.

A doughnut-shaped turnaround at the entrance to the complex reinforces its circularity with a central mound planted in yellow-twig dogwood. Two flagstone "welcome mats" lead to the office buildings. A terrace for the smaller of the two buildings accommodates a bosque of little-leaf lindens, surrounded by a field of plum-colored gravel. Randomly placed gold and gray concrete blocks form a parallelogram-shaped plaza that echoes the shape of CIT's tower building. Near the cafeteria, a dining patio comprises a concrete checkerboard of light and dark pavers.

The original scheme called for planting colored mirror globes in the meadow grasses surrounding the project. The balls were intended to appear as pieces of the building's mirrored facade, scattered like flowers through the grass. The client ultimately decided that the globes couldn't be justified unless they served some purpose. For Schwartz, the elimination of the globes offered a rude awakening into clients' different views toward architecture and landscape architecture. "It was expected that a building could convey an idea or exhibit a radical form, but the landscape was to be the nonintellectual, passive realm in which the building would stand in contrast." She describes this attitude toward landscape as a kind of "environmental fundamentalism, in which people have strong, emotion-based views about landscape, though they know little about it."

Reflection of turnaround at entry

Plan view of entry drop-off and guest parking.

Terrace area adjacent to main hallway and auditorium.

Gazing globes and lines of flagstone seen through gravel and linden bosque.

Open terrace of gravel, stone, and gazing globes.

Rio Shopping Center

Location: *Atlanta, GA*
Client: *Ackerman and Company*
Date: *1988*
Team: *Office of Peter Walker and*
               Martha Schwartz
               Ken Smith
               David Meyer
               Martin Poirier
               Doug Findlay
               David Walker
Architect: *Arquitectonica*
               International
Photography: *Martha Schwartz*
               Rion Rizzo/Creative
               Sources

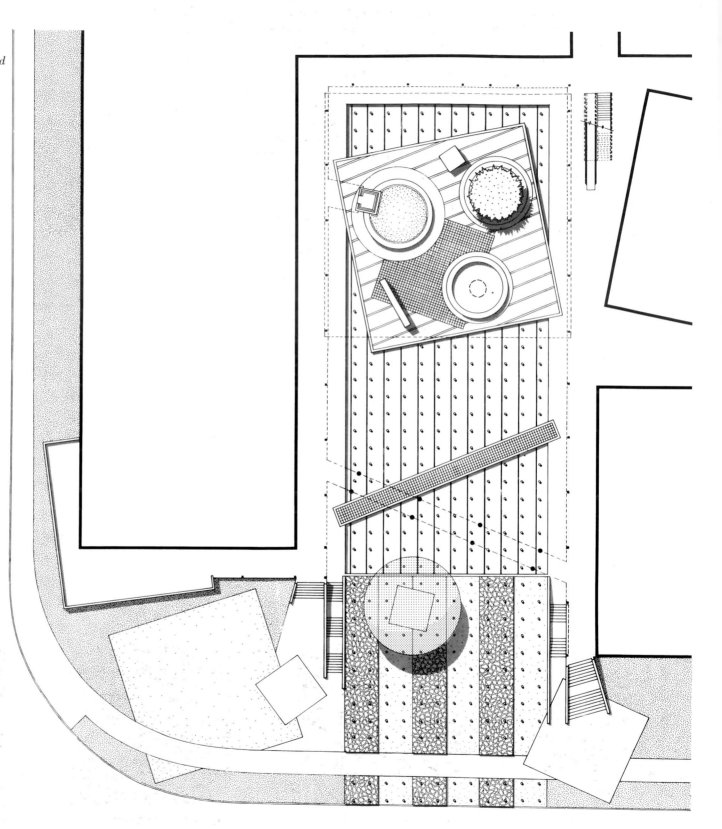

0   40 feet

Site Plan.

A squadron of gilded frogs worships a geodesic globe in the courtyard of a specialty shopping center in midtown Atlanta. Designed by Miami-based architects Arquitectonica, Rio boldly asserts itself among the chaos of a busy intersection in cluttered area ripe for revitalization. The globe serves as a beacon for the retail center, whose first level of shops opens onto the courtyard 10 feet below the street.

Overlapping squares of lawn, paving, stones, and architecture form the basis of the design. The squares are layered with other geometric pieces—lines, circles, spheres, cubes. These elements meet in a mysterious black pool, striated by lines of fiber optics that glow at night.

The frogs are set in a grid at the base of the 40-foot-high globe, stationed on a slope connecting the road to the courtyard. Alternating stripes of riprap and grass blanket the slope; the grid of frogs continues down the slope and through the pool, all facing the giant sphere as if paying homage. The globe, eventually to become a support for kudzu vines, houses a mist fountain. A square plaza beyond this focal point forms a meeting place, housing a circular bar, a bamboo grove that punctures the roof, and a video installation by artist Darra Birnbaum.

A floating path, reflected above by an architectural bridge, connects one side of the shopping area to the other.

View of the kudzu globe and frog pond.

Plan view of the plaza's juice bar/ dance floor.

Frogs and riprap on front lawn.

Street view of the front lawn and kudzu globe.

International Swimming Hall of Fame

Location: Fort Lauderdale, FL
Client: City of Fort Lauderdale
Date: 1987
Team: Office of Peter Walker/
      Martha Schwartz
      Ken Smith
      Gabe Ruspini
Architect: Arquitectonica
           International
Model: Gabe Ruspini
       Ken Smith

Model
Photography: David Walker

The first of many projects to employ bold stripes as a spatial ordering device, the design for the International Swimming Hall of Fame proposes a renovation of an existing swimming facility into a museum, marina, and public park, in collaboration with Arquitectonica. The application of stripes came from an idea inspired by sculptor Carl Andre's minimalist floor pieces, which define a volume of space above a two-dimensional surface. Schwartz explains, "This device is tremendously applicable to landscape, for our means of defining and controlling the landscape rests upon the manipulation of the horizontal plane."

Not only is the ground plane required to organize the existing disparate pieces of the project, it also spans two roads and an existing park, linking the complex to the ocean where swimming races often begin. The ground plane also distinguishes the Hall of Fame from adjacent properties along a seedy segment of highway sprawl.

Stripes, recalling the racing lanes of a swimming pool, unite the 10-acre lawn, pool deck, and parking areas, continuing across the highway and beach to the ocean. The stripes are composed of colored concrete in the parking lots, lanes of grass and ground cover on the lawns, different colored pavers in the pool deck, and sea oats planted in lanes on the beach.

A strong axis, planted in a grove of *Washingtonia* palms, provides a pathway for swimmers to sprint from the ocean to the pools to finish their races.

In the park, an undulating lawn echoes ocean waves, as if the sea had been pumped into the landscape. Mist nozzles create a soft cloud in a fountain of 100 leaping concrete dolphins.

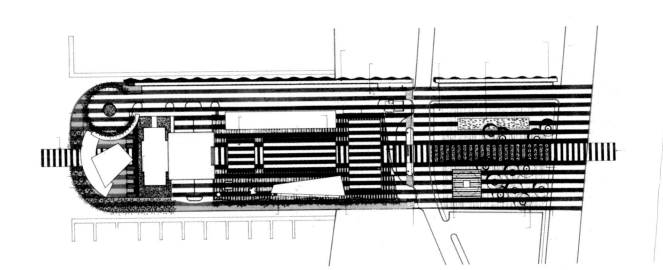

0   300 feet

Aerial view of existing buildings, new "wave" museum, and proposed landscape.

Swimming lane striping extends into the beach; the axis is expressed by an allée of buoys.

Undulating hedge echoes rhythm of undulating canopy.

Undulating lawn flows under existing water tower.

Limed Parterre with Skywriter

Location: Radcliffe Quadrangle
Cambridge, MA

Client: Office for the Arts at
Harvard and Radcliffe

Date: May 1988
Artist: Martha Schwartz
Team: Ken Smith
Photography: Martha Schwartz
David Walker

0   80 feet

Moors Hall is a neoclassical dormitory in the Radcliffe residential quadrangle in Cambridge, Massachusetts. When the building was renovated in 1988, Harvard University commissioned a temporary art piece to celebrate the complete restoration of the quadrangle.

The dormitory, positioned at one end of the rectilinear quadrangle, visually dominates the classically ordered space. At the building's base, a new cafeteria and regrading of the lawn severed the classical relationship of the dormitory to its ground plane. The new construction also destroyed the flatness of the lawn, which formed the connective tissue for all the surrounding buildings on the quadrangle. "Limed Parterre with Skywriter" attempts to return the buildings and landscape of the quadrangle to their classical composition.

In this temporary installation, the six existing "pilasters" on the front of Moors Hall are extended across the cafeteria addition to where they meet the lawn. The lines continue across the length of the lawn in hand-applied lime, cross a parking lot and proceed into the street. Six fog stripes are aligned across the sky parallel to the lawn stripes, describing a room 75 feet wide by 325 feet long by 5,000 feet tall. The sky stripes, repeated several times over a two-hour period, converge at the horizon behind the dormitory, as if the building had generated both lawn and sky stripes. The fog, lime, and paint lines reunite Moors Hall with its classical quadrangle.

Pilasters of Moors Hall are drawn over top of new addition and down to the lawn.

Pilasters are drawn onto the lawn with lime.

Lime lines are drawn over turfed picnic table artwork by Ross Miller.

Turf Parterre Garden

Location:	*World Financial Center Battery Park City, NY*
Client:	*Olympia and York*
Date:	*October 1988*
Artist:	*Martha Schwartz*
Team:	*Ken Smith*
Architect:	*Cesar Pelli*
Photography:	*Robert Walker*
	Lisa Roth

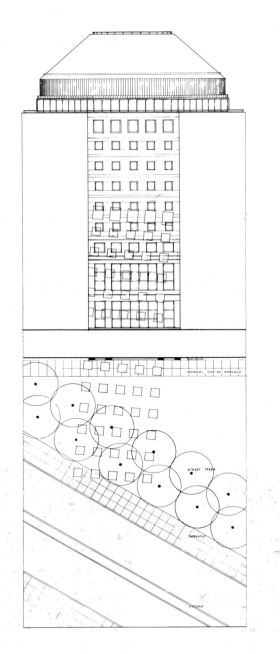

0   50 feet

The Turf Parterre Garden was a temporary art installation conceived as part of "The New Urban Landscape," an exhibition of work by 30 artists and architects marking the completion of the World Financial Center in Lower Manhattan.

The facade of the buildings, designed by architect Cesar Pelli, is distinguished by a point grid pattern of square windows and granite. The intent of the Turf Parterre Garden was to take the architect's facade pattern and reapply it to the building, creating another layer in the form of a garden. Like a strip of patterned Victorian wallpaper, the Parterre Garden rolled out across the lawn in front of the building and up one of its facades, uniting landscape and building. Squares of sod, mirroring the pattern of the windows, were removed from the lawn between the building and the West Side Highway, creating a literal mirror of the building's facade. The pattern continued up the building in the form of artificial turf squares adhered to its surface. In an unexpectedly romantic move, the garden layer was shifted, creating a dissonance between the identical grids of the parterre and the architectural facade. This disturbance functioned in the manner of the ruined perfection of a picturesque garden, in which a fallen temple and fake ruins intentionally disturbed the harmony of the landscape.

Turf parterre wallpaper is applied askew to building grid.

Building facade provides land-scape surface for parterre.

Close-up of Astroturf panels.

Hanging Texas Bluebonnet Field

Location: Robert Mueller
Municipal Airport
Austin, TX

Client: City of Austin
Art in Public Places
Program

Date: 1988 (completed)

Artist: Martha Schwartz

Team: Ken Smith
David Meyer

Photography: Peter Walker
M. Peters

When the City of Austin expanded its 1960s airport in the mid-1980s, Martha Schwartz, Richard Posner, and Jimmy Jalapeno were commissioned as artists to create site-specific outdoor works over 60 acres of utilitarian infrastructure, including the airport's automobile access road, parking lots, drop-off points, and entry plaza. Schwartz's scheme incorporates lines of hedgerows, windbreaks, and allées designed to lead people across parking lots and roads toward the entry. Imposed on the existing landscape, these components were intended to create a new scale of spaces and visual experiences by subdividing the otherwise open field of parking into distinct rooms. A variety of native Texas plants were selected to make each line read separately from the other. Entry to the new terminal building is marked by a 100-foot-square plaza of native limestone paving, heavily planted with local woodland trees in a triangular courtyard at the juncture of old and new buildings. A squadron of plastic flying cactus plants hangs above a formation of plastic armadillos walking on a bed of bright blue gravel.

Inside the airport, upside-down Texas bluebonnets, the state flower, hang from the concrete barrel-vaulted ceiling. The silk bluebonnets, arranged in a line from the front door of the airport through to its single concourse, are hung by a chrome-plated ball chain fastened to the ceiling. Suspended about 3 feet above a traveler's head, the bluebonnets appear to wave in the breeze thanks to the airport's ventilation system.

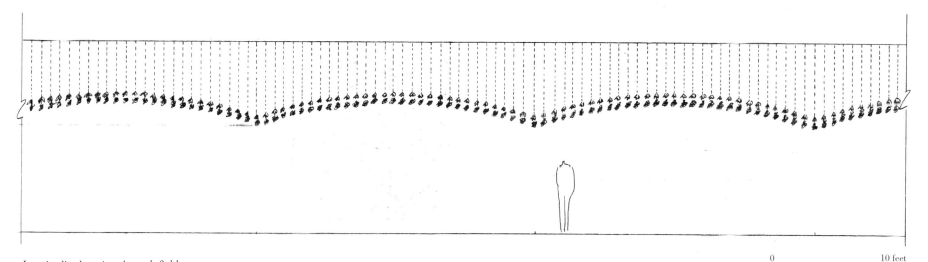

Longitudinal section through field.

0   10 feet

Installation of bluebonnets.

View of upside-down bluebonnets from concourse.

Silk bluebonnets are hung from ceiling by ball-chain.

125

Becton Dickinson
Immunocytometry Division

Location: San Jose, CA
Client: Becton Dickinson
Date: 1990
Team: Schwartz Smith Meyer
                 Ken Smith
                 David Meyer
                 Doug Findlay
                 David Jung
                 Sara Fairchild
Architects: Gensler and Associates
Photography: David Meyer
                 Michael Moran

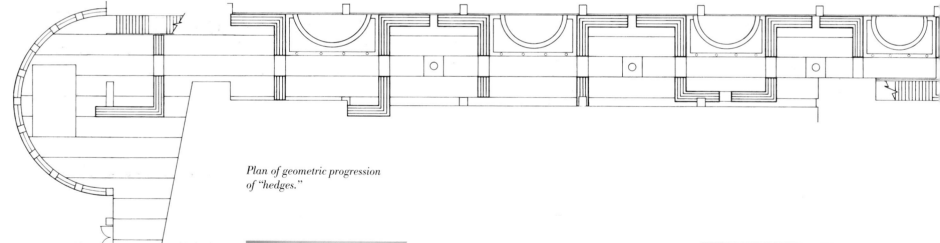

*Plan of geometric progression
of "hedges."*

*A rock and hedge spiral dome sits
in formal vehicular entry.*

*View through "hedge" forms down
hallway.*

A graduated series of 12 garden "rooms" transforms a two-and-a-half story central atrium and 2-acre motor court for a medical research complex in San Jose, California. Defined by "hedges" of wooden armatures planted with ficus vines, the rooms enclose reflecting pools and range in size from 24-foot-square spaces bordered by 16-foot-high "hedges" near the lobby to 4-foot-square, 6-inch-high enclosures at the opposite end of the atrium. The taller, more secluded rooms serve as private conference spaces; the lower-walled spaces offer cafeteria seating. Painted concrete reflecting pools surround ceramic-tile-clad planters containing *Sanseveria*; water pours into the pools from globes along the tiled pool edges, which serve as seating. A fishtail palm colonnade reinforces the atrium's central axis.

The atrium's concrete floor is composed of poured integrally colored concrete in green and black stripes. This pattern extends beyond the building to organize the motor court, where a spiraled rock and ficus dome serve as a focal point.

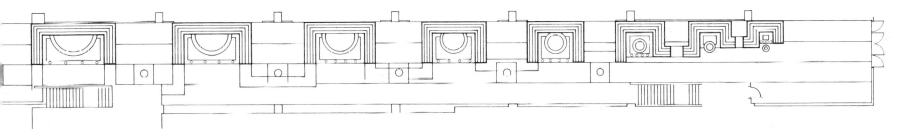

0   40 feet

View from low "hedges," which form smallest "rooms."

View from second floor offices.

Pools change in size as "hedges" progress through atrium.

Ball fountains spit a single jet of water into pool.

New England Holocaust Memorial Competition

Location:	*Boston, MA*
Client:	*New England Holocaust Memorial Committee*
Date:	*1991 (finalist)*
Team:	*Schwartz Smith Meyer*
	Ken Smith
	David Meyer
	Sara Fairchild
	Kathryn Drinkhouse
Computer Graphics:	*France Israel-View by View*

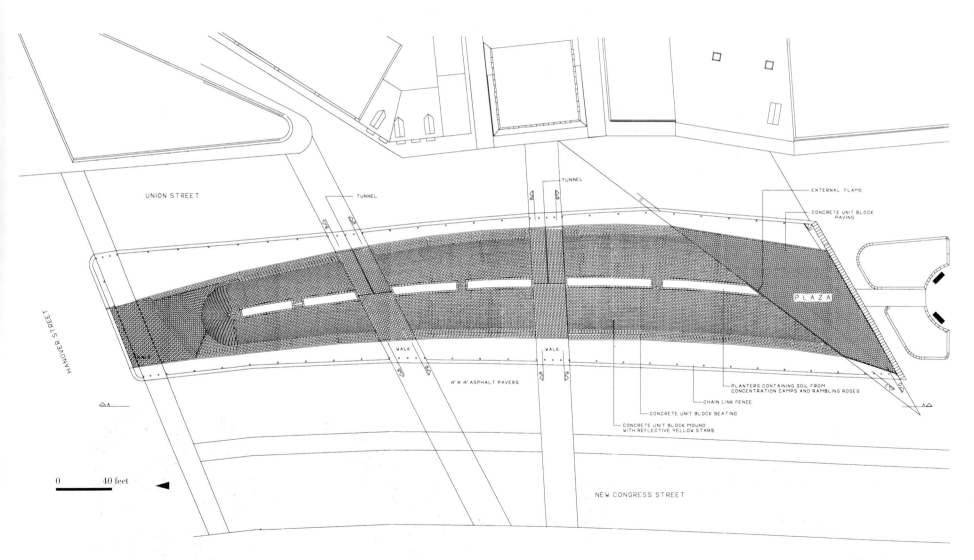

Site plan.

The New England Holocaust Memorial Committee held an open competition for a memorial to be built on a linear traffic island between Boston's City Hall and a block of 18th-century buildings housing the city's oldest restaurants. Because of its site in the midst of major thoroughfares, the memorial design had to be large and simple enough to be experienced from passing cars. A loaflike form, traversed by pedestrian walkway "slices," fills the site. Conceived as an intentionally ambiguous sculptural object, the form can be read as a burial mound, a loaf of bread, or a train.

The mound is composed of 8-by-8-by-16 inch concrete block units and measures 12 feet high, 305 feet long, and 30 to 53 feet wide. It would take 300 such monuments to be able to allocate one concrete block for each person killed in the Holocaust. The blocks are engraved with a Star of David, recalling the arm bands worn by incarcerated Jews. The reflective yellow stars twinkle at night as they are washed by car headlights. Other symbols, such as the pink triangles and brown squares that homosexuals and gypsies were forced to wear, are mixed among the vast field of yellow stars. On the crest of the mound six boxes containing soil from each of the six death camps are planted in *Rosa rugosa*, a white flowering rambling rose.

Crossing through the mound, pedestrians can peer into an 18-inch-diameter tunnel that cuts longitudinally through the mound. As one looks into the opening, millions of minute points of light twinkle in the blackness.

A Kaddish, the Hebrew prayer for the dead, is engraved into the southern wall of the mound. Beside it burns an eternal flame.

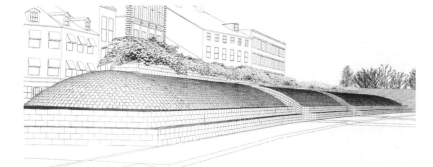

View south of mound.

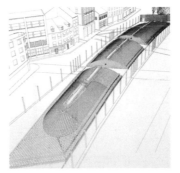

Bird's-eye view of memorial.

Star of David imprinted in concrete block with reflective yellow traffic paint.

Kunsthal Museumpark
Competition

Location: Rotterdam
             The Netherlands
Client: Kunsthal
Date: 1990
Team: Schwartz Smith Meyer
             Ken Smith
             David Meyer
             Sara Fairchild
Architect: Rem Koolhaas

This project was a competition design for the site of a new art museum designed by architect Rem Koolhaas. The new building, adjacent to a 19th-century building and public gardens in Rotterdam, occupies a 2.5-acre site that had to respond to both structures.

A large, sculptural, elliptical mound lies between the 19th- and 20th-century buildings, establishing a mediation between the two formal architectural languages. The 6-foot-high mound is clad in black river stone and visually floats on the surface of a large black reflecting pool, symbolizing the fact that the museum site occupies land reclaimed from the sea. The mound forms a land bridge or island between the two museums; like a museum, it represents an island of culture and art in the more prosaic sea of contemporary city life. Walkways and terraces projecting outward from the buildings intersect with the mound in the form of slices and removals. Existing trees are preserved in tree wells set into the mound.

In contrast to the rectilinear volumes of both buildings, the mound is biomorphic, like a big black beetle or water insect whose back becomes a bridge across the dangerously watery site.

Plan of island, which bridges the existing civic garden and the new museum. Water floods the site.

Section through island reveals wells around existing trees.

Biosphere Competition

Location: *Montreal, Canada*
Client: *City of Montreal*
Date: *1992*
Team: *Schwartz Smith Meyer*
 Ken Smith
 David Meyer
 Sara Fairchild
 Cliff Lowe
Architect: *Griffiths Rankin Cook Architects*
Model: *Griffiths Rankin Cook Architects*

The Biosphere scheme was produced as a competition entry with the Canadian architecture firm of Griffiths Rankin Cook Architects.

The city of Montreal wanted to renovate the dome, designed by Buckminster Fuller, which housed the American Pavilion for the 1967 Montreal Expo. The dome's acrylic skin burned in a spectacular but quick fire in the 1970s. It has remained a ghostly artifact on the Expo '67 site, which occupies an island in the St. Lawrence Seaway.

The competition brief requested that the interior of the dome be renovated to house an ecological museum based on the theme of rivers and water. The design includes a windmill salvaged from Prince Edward Island and placed out on the river, where it pumps gallons of water out of the St. Lawrence and up to the top of the sphere. Here the water enters a purification system that visitors can look into; from this height, the water rains down through displays and water toys and is collected in concentric pools at the base of the sphere. Purified, it finally trickles down through a plaza and eventually empties into the St. Lawrence.

The burning dome.

Model showing interior exhibit space, concentric water circles, and St. Lawrence plaza.

Drawing of landscape plan.

Interior landscape plan for exhibit area.

Los Angeles Center

Location: Los Angeles, CA
Client: Hillman Properties
Date: 1990
Team: Schwartz Smith Meyer
               Ken Smith
               David Meyer
               Sara Fairchild
               Kathryn Drinkhouse
Architect: Johnson Fain Pereira
Model: Sara Fairchild
Model
Photography: Douglas Symes

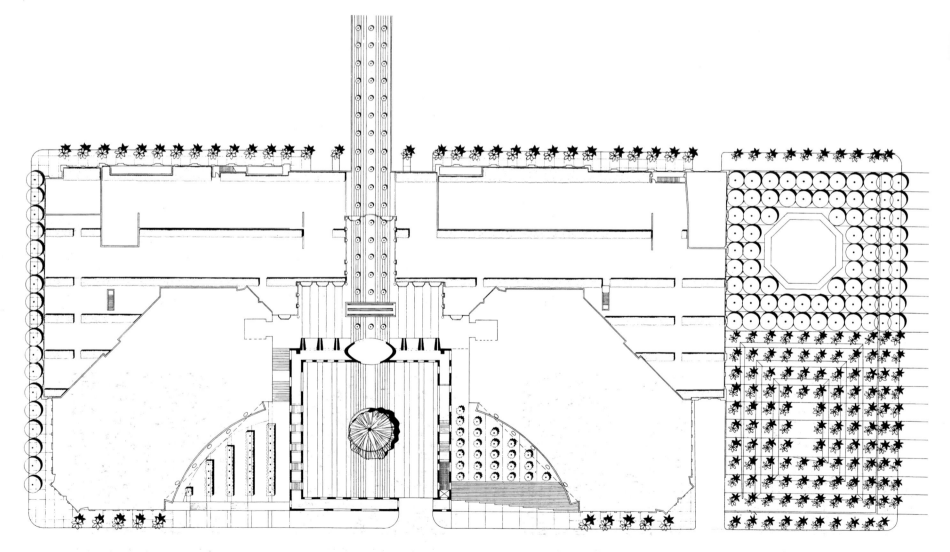

0   100 feet   ▲

Landscape plan for entry plazas,
garage roof, and adjacent public park.

This landscape forms the base of two 40-story office towers by architects Johnson Fain Pereira. Located in downtown Los Angeles, the towers are bridged by a shopping and office complex.

The site presented a grading challenge: the area in front of the buildings occupies a pronounced slope, requiring the buildings' lobbies to be located on three different levels. A motor court, connected by a ramp to an underground parking garage, functions as a grand entry area, establishing the street image of the complex.

A giant outdoor room is described by a 10,000-square-foot box enclosed by four walls of Indian sandstone. This box forms the entry courtyard, flanked to the north and south by entry plazas to the two office towers. The elevation of this room responds to the ground floor of the center of the complex and to the street level, enabling cars to drop off passengers and enter the garage. A second, larger box, also of sandstone, surrounds the inner box of the motor courtyard, resolving the grade differences between courtyard and north and south plazas.

The two 25-foot-tall concentric walls form a slot of space, 6 feet wide, conceived as a moat. Recalling the pre-Los Angeles, Pleistocene landscape of the La Brea tar pits, the "crack" between the walls contains a swamp, glimpsed from cars on the street through a series of low windows formed in the wall, through the openings in the wall at the car entry, or as one crosses the moat when ascending or descending steps to an adjacent plaza.

Interior walls facing the swamp are surfaced in bands of fritted green and blue glass to give the slot a watery effect.

Opposing lines of 1/2-inch-diameter stainless steel pipe extend 5 inches from each wall, delivering drops of water to the swamp. The sound of these dripping fountains fills the space. Growlights are located within one of the glass bands to light the swamp plants.

The car entry courtyard is planted with a singular 60-foot-tall *Washingtonia* palm. This palm is a symbol of Los Angeles, and of the Los Angeles Center. In order to emphasize the importance of this plant, it is encircled by a 3-foot-diameter concrete ring surfaced in lead shingles.

In keeping with the primitive plant palette, the north plaza is planted with a grove of bottle palms (*Beaucarnea recurvata*). This odd, sculptural plant will help draw pedestrian traffic up the stairs to the plaza. The south plaza is planted with dragon trees (*Dracaena draco)*, which could also be imagined to have inhabited Pleistocene Los Angeles.

0   40 feet

Aerial view of main entry court and vehicular drop-off enclosed by concentric boxes made of sandstone walls.

View of singular palm, surrounded by ring surfaced in lead shingles.

View from street into slot garden enclosed by sandstone walls.

Steps linking plazas traverse moat, allowing pedestrians a view into swamp environment.

Columbia Center

Location: Chicago, IL
Client: Fifield Development Corporation
Date: 1990
Team: Schwartz Smith Meyer
     Ken Smith
     David Meyer
     Sara Fairchild
     Jeffrey Smith
Architect: DeStefano/Goetsch, Architects
Model: Ken Smith
     Jeffrey Smith
Model
Photography: Ken Smith
     Doug Cogger

Columbia Center is an office complex located among hotels and other airport outbuilding sprawl around Chicago O'Hare. The design by architects DeStefano/Goetsch of Chicago is an introverted group of buildings that focus on their own courtyard. This courtyard is used by people who work in the buildings, diners from an adjacent cafeteria, and, most of all, by office workers whose windows overlook it from surrounding buildings.

The architects asked for a scheme that required excavating below the first level to give basement offices a courtyard view. Rather than propose the expense of excavating the entire area, Schwartz's scheme scoops out four quadrants, leaving a cruciform mound in the center. The four-part garden is based on a traditional Indian and Islamic concept: the quadrants symbolize the four corners of the earth and are rendered in red, yellow, black, and white materials. A shallow pool of blue marbles and water at the top of the mound represents life and unifies the project. The project was dropped due to the recession in 1992.

Plan of garden symbolizing the four corners of the world. "Water" ties the four corners to each other.

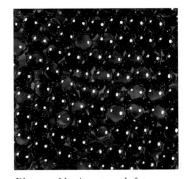

Blue marbles in a trough form a symbolic year-round "water element."

The white garden contains paper birches and limestone.

The black garden is composed of anthracite, asphalt, and Liriope.

The yellow garden is composed of yellow sandstone, yellow-twig dogwoods, and bird baths.

The red garden is composed of red granite, birch, and purple plum trees.

Moscone Center Competition

Location: *San Francisco, CA*
Client: *San Francisco Arts Commission*
Date: *1990 (placed second)*
Artist: *Martha Schwartz*
Team: *Ken Smith*
           David Meyer
           Sara Fairchild
Model: *Ken Smith*
           Sara Fairchild

Howard Street in San Francisco's former warehouse district is flanked by the Moscone Convention Center to the west and Yerba Buena Center—a cultural complex of gardens, a theater, and museums—to the east. A new addition to the Moscone Center forms Yerba Buena's westernmost edge. The 250-by-250-foot Howard Street Plaza links the convention center with its annex and adjacent cultural complex. The design addresses the complexities of the site by creating an identifiable "welcome mat" to unify the disparate architectural elements surrounding the plaza.

The imagery of the plaza is borrowed from the American tradition of quilting. The metaphor symbolizes the "stitching together" of discrete pieces to create something of lasting beauty and value. The crazy quilt plaza also represents San Francisco's diverse mosaic of neighborhoods, people, and cultures. Constructed of colored concrete stamped with a patterned mold during construction, the quilt enlivens the street, which remains open to vehicles, between Yerba Buena and the Moscone center. The concrete material, which is typically applied to imitate stone or finer paving, is used here for what it is—an inexpensive, engaging material. A yellow-painted striped walkway drawn on the surface of the quilt directs foot traffic across the street at ground level.

Existing site in front of Moscone Center.

Aerial view of "crazy quilt" plaza and painted pedestrian crosswalk spanning the street.

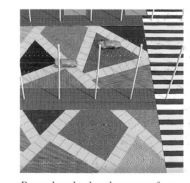

Pressed and colored concrete form patches of quilt.

Fukuoka International Housing

Location: Fukuoka, Japan
Client: Fukuoka Jisho Company, Ltd.
Date: 1990 (partial completion)

Team: Schwartz Smith Meyer
Ken Smith
David Meyer
Kathryn Drinkhouse
Scott Summers
Verda Alexander
Architect: Mark Mack
Photography: Richard Barnes
Martha Schwartz

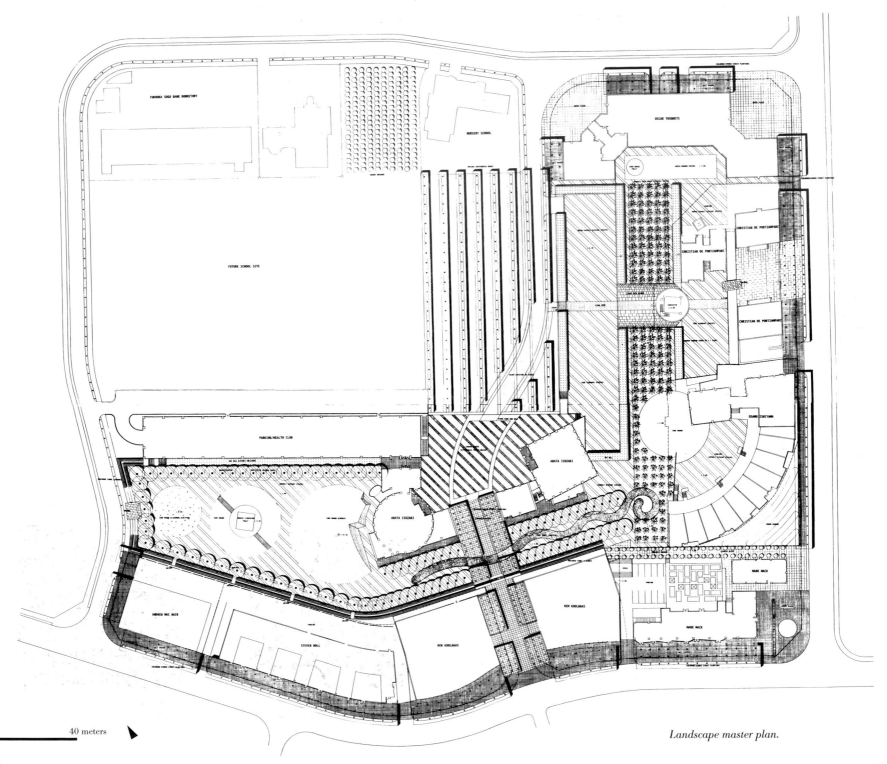

0   40 meters

Landscape master plan.

Fukuoka, in southern Japan, is the site of a housing complex constructed in the mid-1980s to showcase the work of eight internationally respected architects. Residential towers and apartment blocks have been designed by Arata Isosaki, Mark Mack, Andrew MacNair, Rem Koolhaas, Steven Holl, Osamu Ishiyama, Oscar Tusquets, and Christian de Portzamparc. The site also includes follies by Zaha Hadid and Daniel Liebeskind, and an elementary school by Alvaro Siza. Schwartz was asked to create a park that would unify the distinct architectural styles of the eleven participating design architects, while also giving the 22,000-square-meter complex a memorable identity.

A "tablecloth underlying the objects in a still life painting" metaphorically describes the continuous, patterned ground plane, rendered in a variety of materials including grass, gravel, and asphalt. Because the spaces around the buildings had a leftover quality, Schwartz sought to unify the scraps with a series of strong landscape forms. In the region bounded by Rem Koolhaas's and Steven Holl's buildings, three grassy hemispheres, graduated in size and recalling burial mounds, protrude from the ground plane. Schwartz approached the project as an exploration of the landfill upon which the complex is built: "I wanted to express the fact that Fukuoka is constructed on artificial ground that carries within it fragments of people's lives and materials brought from elsewhere." A palm grove behind buildings by Tusquets and Portzamparc is designed as a simple backdrop to their rather complicated facades. The palm court creates a communal outdoor room and provides much-needed shade. The Japanese initially resisted the palms because they associate them with the beach, vacation, and fun; Schwartz's vision that even home can be fun prevailed.

Mark Mack's Fukuoka building occupies a corner site at a prominent entrance to the housing complex. Built on landfill, the site includes a roof garden atop a semi-underground parking structure and a plaza at the base of Mack's tower. A domed earth form covered with ceramic tile protrudes from beneath the tiled surface of the plaza, suggesting a man-made object rising out of the earth. Mist rises from a grated "crack," as though the earth were undergoing chemical transformations and venting. On the roof deck, a series of concrete-block boxes are designed for residents to plant with vegetables or flowers.

Mist flows from grated "crack" fountain.

Dome surfaced in kawara tile occupies corner site.

Raised beds of earth provide vegetable gardens for tenants.

Plan view of vegetable gardens on roof of garage.

Dickenson Residence

Location: *Santa Fe, NM*
Client: *Nancy Dickenson*
Date: *1991-1992*
Team: *Schwartz Smith Meyer*
                David Meyer
                Sara Fairchild
                Ken Smith
Architect: *Steven Jacobson*
Photography: *Martha Schwartz*

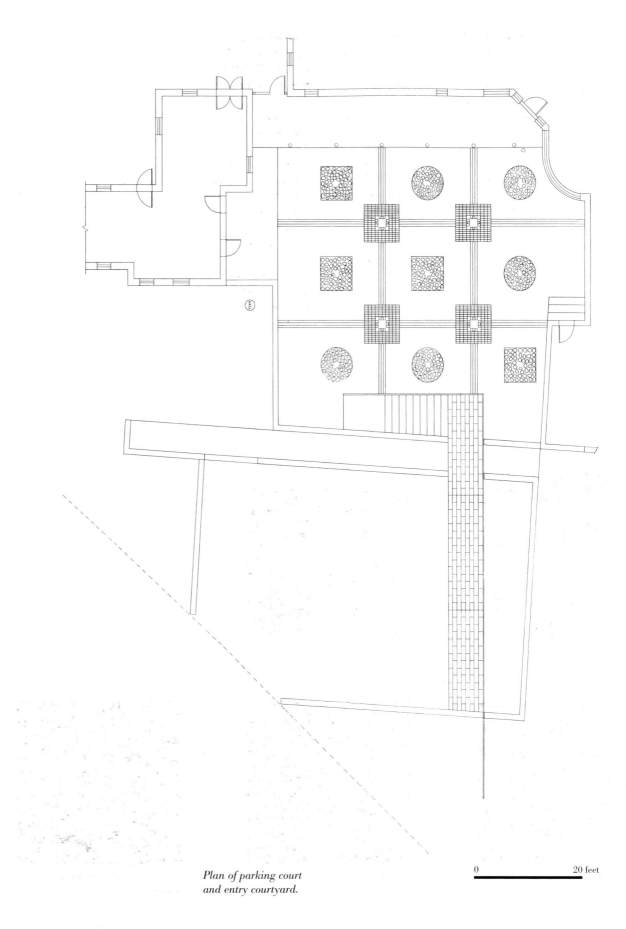

*Plan of parking court
and entry courtyard.*

0 ———————— 20 feet

Nancy Dickenson is a collector of folk art whose adobe house is situated on 20 acres of mesa landscape north of Santa Fe. Visiting the property, Schwartz observed that the existing processional through the house forced visitors through a garage, utility room, private study, and kitchen before finally reaching the entrance and living room, which opened onto views of the Sangre de Christo Mountains. A series of landscape rooms were designed to grow progressively more intimate, creating a processional from the exterior world into the inner sanctum.

Schwartz's scheme also counters the ubiquitous organic form of Santa Fe-style adobe houses. Introducing a series of structured events defined by a clear geometry, she brings a sense of orientation to the existing plan. However, because it seemed impossible to make a believable transition between a garden and the existing landscape of exposed soil, juniper, and pinyon pine, she enclosed all the new plantings and structures within walls.

Visitors arrive at an auto court, then proceed to a sunken courtyard, where a grid of fountains and runnels encloses nine flowering crabapple trees. White marble boulders under the trees suggest exaggerated gravel. Four square brick fountains are lined with brightly colored metal panels that enhance the water's sound. The pool area is spare by contrast, a platform from which to view the landscape. Terraced in Arizona sandstone, the eye is directed toward the mountains. Outside the client's bedroom, a grassy roof terrace gestures toward the view.

View from pool area to mountains.

Top of new pool house provides an opportunity to use turf as an extension of main bedroom.

Four brick fountains organize courtyard.

Tiled runnels deliver water into wells.

Painted steel sleeves create colored light.

Lit stair leads from parking court down into sunken entry courtyard.

The Citadel

Location: Commerce, CA
Client: Trammell Crow Company
Date: 1991
Team: Schwartz Smith Meyer
               Ken Smith
               David Meyer
               Sara Fairchild
               Kathryn Drinkhouse
Architect: The Nadel Partnership
               Sussman Prejza
Photography: Marc Treib
               Jay Venezia
               Martha Schwartz
               David Meyer

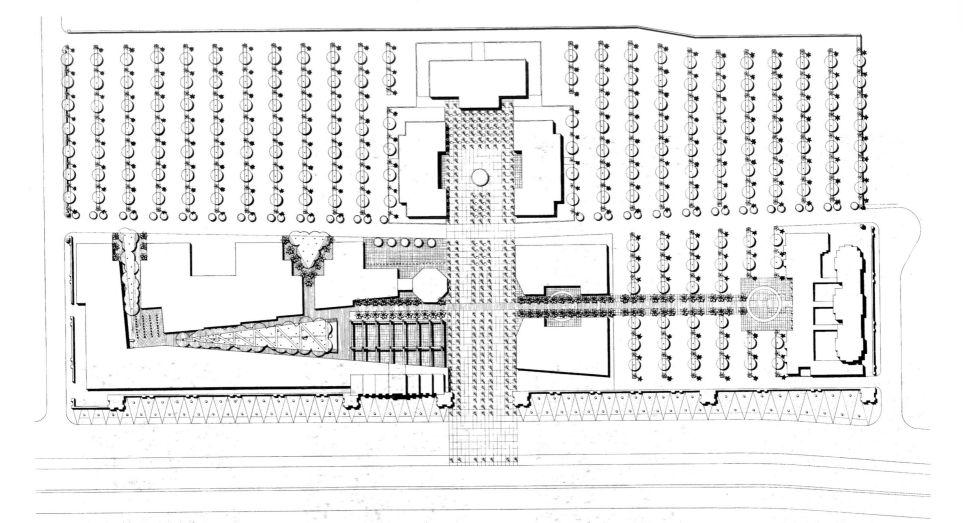

0   200 feet

Site plan.

Schwartz master-planned this 35-acre property in Commerce, California, the former site of the Uniroyal Tire and Rubber Company's Middle Eastern-style factory built in 1929. The developer of the site preserved the Assyrian-temple-inspired front wall of the factory's exterior but demolished its remainder to make room for four office buildings, a retail mall, and a hotel. In such mixed-use developments, the conventional wisdom calls for buildings to be sited equidistant from parking, but Schwartz ignored this prescription and arranged the buildings around a central plaza. She also bravely cut a 150-foot swath out of the wall itself, creating a grand spatial sweep through the complex that directs cars to two large parking lots at its eastern end.

The plaza is defined by a 150-foot-by-700-foot oasis of date palms: "The idea was to create a great central allée that became everybody's front yard," explains Schwartz. Tire-shaped rings—Schwartz calls them the "ghosts of tires past"—surround the palms. The rings serve as seating at lunchtime and also protect the trees from cars. Schwartz designed this allée for pedestrians and automobiles, clearly delegating primacy to the former. Eschewing conventional roadway elements such as curbs and gutters, she aligned the concrete tires to direct traffic, allowing pedestrians to freely penetrate the plaza.

Existing site formerly owned by Uniroyal Tire Company.

Existing office building of Uniroyal Tire Company.

Grand allée of date palms surrounded by concrete tires.

Paving is constructed of single concrete block pavers.

Concrete tires recall the tires once manufactured on the site.

Central allée allows vehicles but is foremost a plaza for pedestrians.

Concrete tires serve as seating so people can wander from adjacent food court to sit and eat.

Snoopy's Garden

Location: Ito, Japan
Client: Landor Associates
Date: 1991
Team: Schwartz Smith Meyer
               Ken Smith
               David Meyer
Architect: Kobe/Ou Design
Computer
Graphics: France Israel-View by View

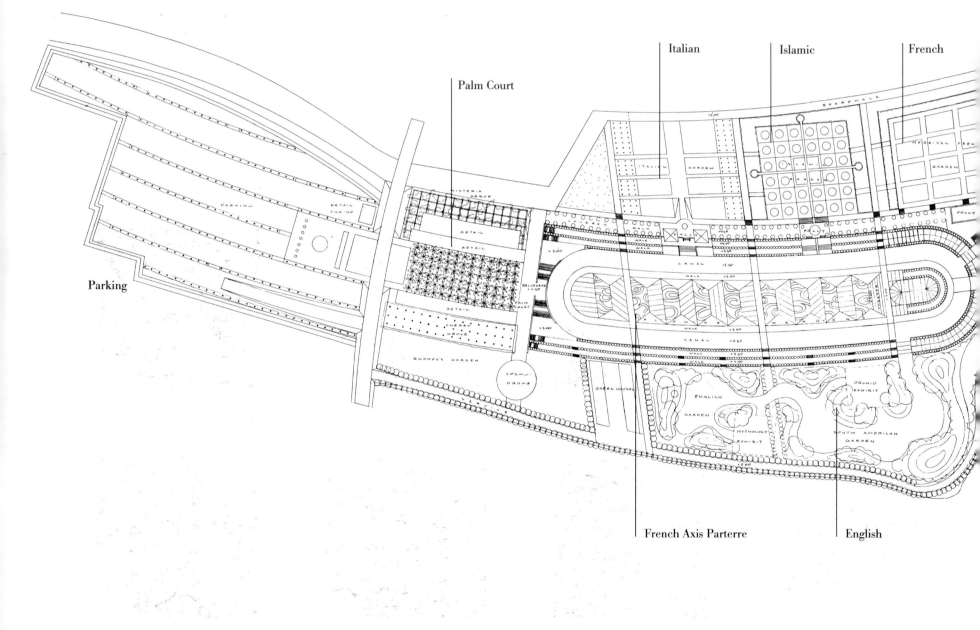

Italian   Islamic   French

Palm Court

Parking

French Axis Parterre   English

0   20 meters   ▲

Master plan of site.

The client, a successful cut-flower merchant, owned 40 acres of land in Ito, an hour north of Tokyo, where he hoped to establish a theme park dedicated to gardens around the world, in which he could display his flowers. Along with the various gardens, the program included parking, a huge court flanked by buildings for concessions, restaurants, meeting rooms, and an outdoor entertainment area with an amphitheater.

Schwartz created a site plan for a complex that would function as a museum. To create a strong orientation and organization, the team suggested a French renaissance-style axis as a major hallway and gathering place. Off this east-west corridor, arranged in an enfilade, are the various "rooms" containing Islamic, Italian, French, Chinese, and English gardens.

This French axis contains a canal flanked on both sides by walkways. Marching down the axis are a series of engineered land forms that rise steeply to 15 feet. These folded landforms have either a baroque or minimalist hedge and flower parterre on either side; their angled sides allow visitors to see the flowers more easily, much as one views fruits and vegetables in a grocery store.

Surrounding lowlands are planted in ornamental grasses. Because the owner had acquired the use of Snoopy as a symbol for his cut flowers, a very large Snoopy is drawn into the flood plain in ornamental grasses.

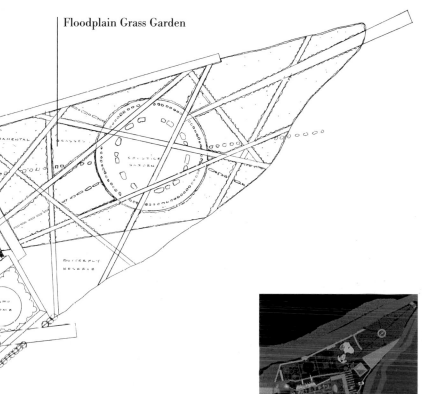

Floodplain Grass Garden

Site plan.

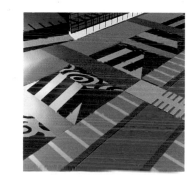

Folded mounds reinforce French axis.

Meandering boat ride through English garden.

Baroque parterre side of folded mounds.

Aerial view of minimal parterre side of folded mounds.

Aerial view from parking area, across highway to palm court.

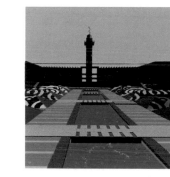

View down central water channel to exhibit and auditorium building.

HUD Plaza Improvements

Location: *Washington, D.C.*
Client: *General Services Administration and Department of Housing and Urban Development*
Date: *1996-97*

Team: Martha Schwartz, Inc.
          Evelyn Bergaila
          Paula Meijerink
          Chris Macfarlane
          Michael Blier
          Kevin Conger
          Sara Fairchild
          Scott Wunderle
          Kaki Martin
          David Bartsch
          Rick Casteel

Architect: Architrave, P.C.
Computer Graphics: Rick Casteel

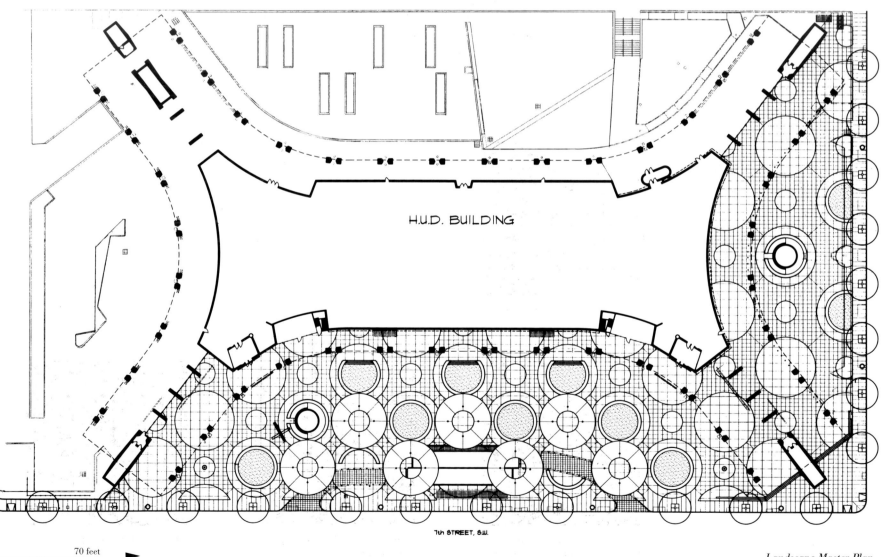

H.U.D. BUILDING

7th STREET, S.W.

0 ——————— 70 feet ▶

Landscape Master Plan

Although Marcel Breuer's 1968 building for the Department of Housing and Urban Development (HUD) in Washington, D.C., bears a richly textured facade, its 6-acre plaza is clearly a casualty of the modernist esthetic. Without trees or public amenities, the plaza was designed to showcase the building but is virtually unusable by HUD's 4,800 employees. Adding to the desolation of this landscape is the fact that the base of the building is a solid wall of dark stone that prohibits a visual connection between the life of the building within and without. Martha Schwartz was commissioned to reactivate HUD's plaza with a new design that would express the agency's mission—creating habitable spaces for people.

Schwartz's scheme repeats a circular motif in vermilion, yellow, and cobalt blue, recalling Breuer's own color palette and geometric designs for screens, walls, and ceilings. The plaza is transformed through a painted ground plane, a series of concrete planters containing grass, and boldly colored doughnut-shaped canopies. The 30-foot-diameter planters double as seating; the canopies, fabricated of vinyl-coated plastic fabric, are raised 18 feet above the ground plane on steel poles. The canopies and planters appear to float, in sharp contrast to the heaviness and somberness of the architecture. The canopies also provide shade on a plaza that was not designed to support the soil required for trees.

Lit from within, the canopies glow at night, recalling the lanterns that illuminate paths in Japanese gardens. A fiber-optic tube casts colored light under the planters, making them appear to float on a cloud of light.

On the building's wall, a backlit photographic mural reflects the people and faces of HUD, creating a dramatic backdrop for the plaza.

Eighteen-inch-high planters visually float above plaza surface.

Bullnose concrete perimeter of planters provides seating.

Canopies offer a sense of shelter and relief from the gaze of office workers above.

Translucent vinyl canopies appear to glow at night.

Canopies hover over the surface of the plaza, supported by stainless steel poles.

Davis Residence

Location: *El Paso, TX*
Client: *Sam and Anne Davis*
Date: *1996*
Team: *Martha Schwartz, Inc.*
         Michael Blier
         Sara Fairchild
         Kevin Conger
         Paula Meijerink

Computer
Graphics: *Rick Casteel*

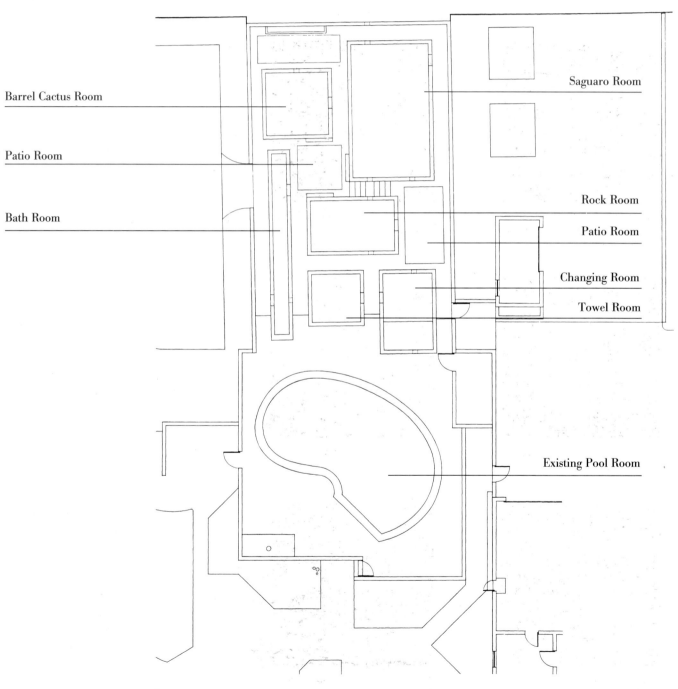

Barrel Cactus Room

Patio Room

Bath Room

Saguaro Room

Rock Room

Patio Room

Changing Room

Towel Room

Existing Pool Room

0   20 feet

In El Paso, Texas, horticulturist Anne Davis created an English garden oasis in a tough desert environment. She offered Schwartz a 37-by-60-foot walled area on her property in which to create whatever the landscape architect wished. However, Anne Davis wanted a Mexican-style garden that would also require little maintenance. "I loved the challenge of creating a garden in a certain style, and viewed the assignment as building a folly in the English garden," Schwartz explains. Because it was contained, the folly could be autonomous from everything going on outside its walls. Her design comprises a series of gardens inside garden "rooms," a metaphor for a house. Plantings of different cacti inhabit the various rooms, whose interiors and exteriors are ambiguous—the outside of one room forms the inside of another. Stucco walls are painted alternately in intense bright and deep somber colors.

Aerial view of garden reveals spatial relationship of six boxlike "rooms" within perimeter walls.

Corridor between "bathroom" box and "rock room."

Interior of mirrored "changing room."

View into "Saguaro room."

Glass chunks mark top of "bath room" walls.

View through trellis canopy into "pool room" with wall of nails.

147

Jacob Javits Plaza

Location: New York, NY
Client: U.S. General Services Administration, HUD
Date: 1996-97 (completion)
Team: Martha Schwartz, Inc.
Laura Rutledge
Maria Bellalta
Chris Macfarlane
Michael Blier
Leo Jew

Computer
Images: Rick Casteel

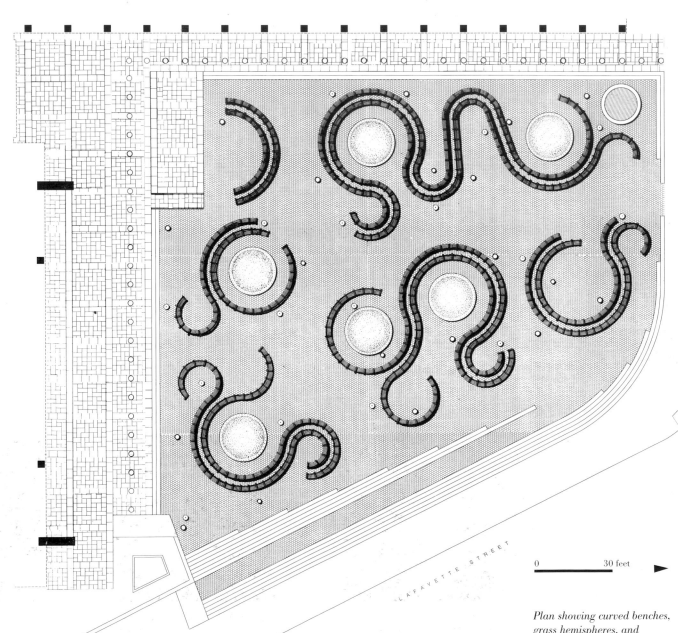

WORTH STREET

LAFAYETTE STREET

0   30 feet

Plan showing curved benches, grass hemispheres, and reconfiguration of the site.

Jacob Javits Plaza, which skirts a 1967 federal office tower in lower Manhattan, was the site of Richard Serra's controversial "Tilted Arc." The 14-foot-high sculpture obstructed the plaza and interrupted pedestrian flow; for several years, Serra fought growing public pressure to have the piece removed. In 1987, the artist lost a legal battle against the General Services Administration (GSA), which sponsored the project, and the piece was dismantled. The removal of "Tilted Arc" created a physical hole in the plaza as well as a breached sense of trust between artists and the GSA.

Because the plaza is in the heart of Manhattan's civic district, it is liveliest during the weekday lunch hour. After the sculpture was removed, workers in the federal office building placed temporary benches and planters across the plaza. Nevertheless, the same dreary conditions to which Serra had so strongly responded prevailed: the plaza was cut off from Lafayette Street by its height and from Worth Street by planters and a fountain. The building demonstrated the prevailing modernist site-planning wisdom of placing a tower in a large featureless plaza. Trees were seen as competing forms that might hinder views of the building, so the plaza was not designed to support them.

Schwartz reconnects the plaza to the orthogonal grid of the city by removing the large planters at the northwest and southeast corners of the site. She also removes the empty fountain from the northernmost corner, opening up the only sunny part of the plaza for seating.

Required to retain a flat surface for reasons of safety and accessibility, Schwartz energizes the plaza with complex forms and color, much as the French elevated a simple flat plane with clipped hedges, grass, and gravel. French *parterres embroideries* were a device often used to energize flat open spaces. They were frequently punctuated by topiary forms, and their edges were defined by trees and buildings. Javits Plaza's "hedges" are twisting strands of New York City park benches. The double strands of back-to-back benches loop back and forth and allow for a variety of seating—intimate circles for groups and flat outside curves for those who wish to lunch alone.

The benches swirl around the "topiary"—6-foot-tall grassy hemispheres that exude mist on hot days. Familiar lunchtime paraphernalia—blue-enameled drinking fountains, Central Park light stands, and orange wire-mesh trash cans—occupy the plaza surface. These elements offer a critique of the art of landscape in New York City, where the ghost of Frederick Law Olmsted is too great a force for even New York to exorcise. Although the city remains a cultural mecca for most art forms, exploration in landscape architecture receives little support. Javits Plaza is therefore a recognizable park, historic and acceptable to New Yorkers, but its familiar elements have all gone a little mad.

Existing site after removal of "Tilted Arc."

Baroque parterre is the model for the design.

Standard New York park benches are arranged in double-sided twisting strands.

The continuous twisting and winding of the benches provides a great variety of seating choices.

Plan view of double-sided benches shows standard acorn light fixture with exaggerated long pole.

World Cup 1994

Location: 12 Sites in the U.S.
Client: World Cup USA
Date: Summer 1994
Team: Martha Schwartz, Inc.
               Maria Bellalta
               Leo Jew
Photography: Maria Bellalta

Working as part of a design team that included graphic designers and advertising consultants, Schwartz was commissioned to invent an image for the sites where the World Cup soccer games were to be held in 12 different cities around the United States. A generic, temporary landscape that could be applied to the different stadiums was conceived. Composed of easily removable and reusable elements, the landscape could not permanently impact the site.

Graphics for the World Cup, developed by graphic designer Cliff Selbert, became the basis for the landscapes. The program called for creating seating; a clear, obvious path to the stadium from the parking area; and a way of marking the location of concessions. Two generic parterres were invented as patterns for painting the vast amount of asphalt typically outside stadiums. These parterres, either checkerboard patterns or wavy stripes, indicated areas of entry or passage. "Tree tents," shaped like elongated pyramids, were constructed of fabric and placed in "groves." They could be arranged to function in numerous ways, either to mark the pedestrian path to the parking area or to signify a precinct of concession stands. A series of "wavy tooth" benches, fabricated from fiberglass and upholstered with Astroturf, represented a three-dimensional interpretation of one of the games' graphic symbols.

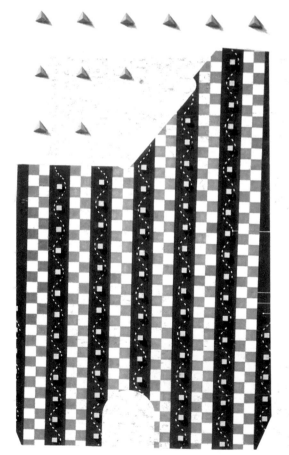

Generic landscape #1 with painted asphalt in a checkerboard pattern, "tree tents," and Astroturf boxes for seating.

Generic landscape #2 with painted asphalt in a wavy pattern, "tree tents," and wavy tooth benches.

Painted checkerboard and asphalt plaza.

"Tree tents" can be easily moved to form bosques and allées to enhance wayfinding.

Wavy tooth benches are surfaced in Astroturf.

The Littman Wedding

Location: Deal, NJ
Client: Barbara and
            Leonard Littman
Date: September 17, 1995
Team: Martha Schwartz, Inc.
            Kevin Conger
            Kaki Martin
            Paula Meijerink
            Michael Blier
Photography: Michael Blier

The one-third-acre Littman residence in Deal on the New Jersey shore was in the process of being dismantled for a new, permanent garden being designed by Schwartz. The transitional state of the landscape allowed the team great freedom in constructing a temporary garden for the wedding of the Littmans' son. "We could paint the grass or the concrete, because we knew we would be tearing it up" for the permanent landscape installation, Schwartz explains.

Since both bride and groom love gardening, "the garden" was the wedding's thematic focus. A series of event spaces were designed to accompany the choreography of the wedding.

A. The Long Walkway with Handsome Men
Two rows of 60 8-foot-tall arborvitae line a 150-foot-long Astroturf walkway arranged along the existing gravel driveway. The walkway passes through a field of empty flowerpots, painted blue on the inside, which mark the entrance to the ceremony tent and refer to the ocean view beyond.

B. The Ceremony
In a simple white tent, the ceremony takes place with the ocean as backdrop. Candles and black-eyed Susans in pots surround the bride and groom.

C. The Reception
The existing pool deck is transformed by a painted pattern of random yellow circles that overlap the patio and lawn.

D. The Banquet
A 50-by-100-foot white tent houses a field of white-clothed tables set in lines, as in a Bruegel painting. Potted orange trees, their foliage trimmed into balls at eye level, are arranged in rows in the center of the tables, blocking guests' view of the room when they first enter it. When seated, the guests can easily see the whole space and feel the enclosure of the overhead tree canopy. The roots of each tree are exposed, potted in clear, 12-inch-diameter acrylic cylinders that run down the center of the table.

E. The Sunflower Grove
A strolling garden was designed as a transitional space that guests walk through between events. The existing gravel, concrete, and grass surfaces are transformed by overlaying a 40-foot square of purple paint. A grid of 5-foot-tall bundled sunflowers is anchored in pots and placed on the purple grass.

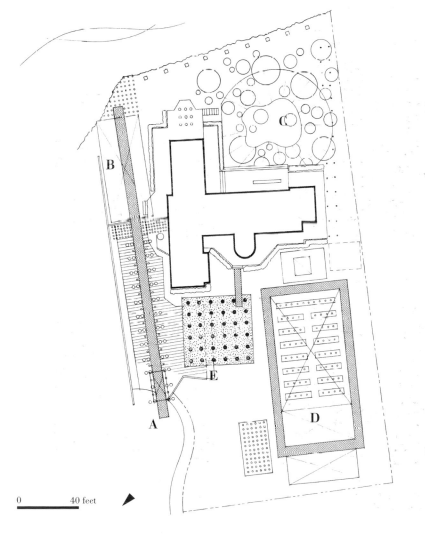

0   40 feet

Astroturf walkway leads the bride and groom through a field of flowerpots with blue interiors.

Yellow circles are painted on the concrete surface around the pool.

A bosque of citrus trees sits on a carpet of painted grass.

A grid of cut sunflowers placed in flowerpots sits on a carpet of purple painted grass.

Federal Courthouse Plaza

Location: Minneapolis, MN
Client: U.S. General Services
                   Administration
Architect: Kohn Pedersen Fox
                   Associates Architects
Date: 1998 completion
Team: Martha Schwartz, Inc.
                   Paula Meijerink
                   Chris Macfarlane
                   Laura Rutledge
                   Maria Bellalta
                   Leo Jew
Model: Maria Bellalta
                   Leo Jew
Model
Photography: Maria Bellalta

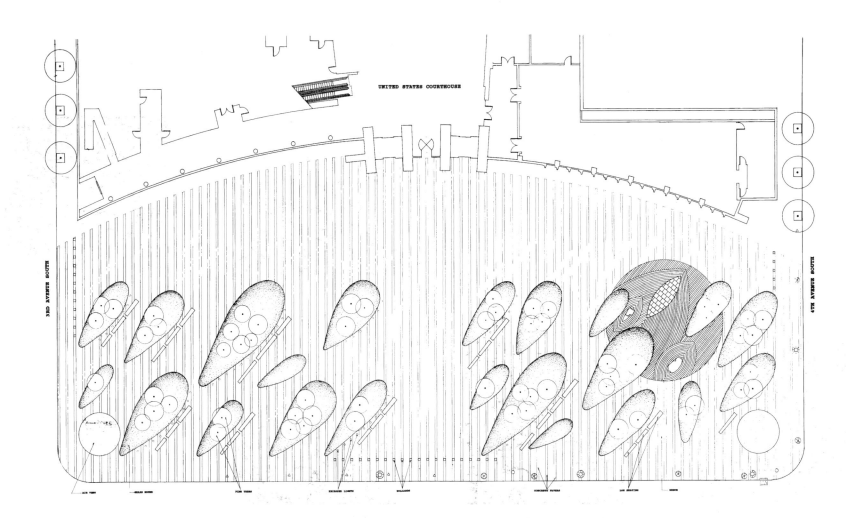

0   40 feet

Plan view of plaza showing mounds,
jack pine, and circular fountain.

The 50,000-square-foot plaza is located in Minneapolis's civic center, facing city hall and in front of a new federal courthouse designed by Kohn Pedersen Fox. The program required a plaza designed for both civic and individual activities, with its own imagery and sense of place.

Earth mounds and logs, elements of Minnesota's cultural and natural history, are the plaza's symbolic and sculptural elements. These components symbolize both the natural landscape and man's manipulation of it for his own purposes.

The mounds are intended to evoke a memory of geological and cultural forms; they might suggest a field of glacial drumlins, a stylized hill region, or, like a Japanese garden, a landscape that allows a dual reading of scale—a range of mountains or a low field of mounds. Rising to a height of 7 feet, the tear-shaped mounds

are planted with jack pine, a small, stunted, pioneer species common in Minnesota's boreal forest. The logs, evocative of the great timber forests that attracted immigrants and provided the basis for the local economy, tell a similar story. The association of timber with Minnesota speaks to the heart of Minnesotans' collective memory.

Typical drumlin landform found in central Minnesota.

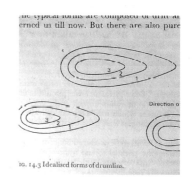

Diagram of typical drumlin topography.

Model of plaza, mounds, trees, and logs.

Plaza sits between new federal courthouse building and old city hall.

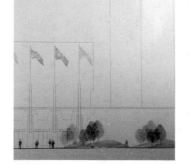

View of plaza looking north.

Baltimore Inner Harbor Competition

In Association with Design Collective, Inc.

Location: *Baltimore Inner Harbor--*
                        West Shore, Baltimore, MD

Client: *Baltimore Development*
                        Corporation

Date: *1993-96 (Phase I completed)*

Team: *Martha Schwartz, Inc.*
                        Maria Bellalta, Leo Jew,
                        Laura Rutledge

Architect: *Design Collective, Inc.*

Model: *Design Collective, Inc., and*
                        Martha Schwartz, Inc.

Phase I: Conway Street Plaza and Welcome Center Plaza

Team: *Martha Schwartz, Inc.*
                        Evelyn Bergaila, Paula Meijerink,
                        Michael Blier, Chris Macfarlane
                        Kevin Conger, Kaki Martin

Competition-winning plan.

0   200 feet ▶

Plan view of competition entry.

Aerial view of grassed berms of "blue crab" park.

View to natural history spiral and skating rink from vantage point of Federal hill.

Natural history spiral brings cultural and natural histories of water's edge together.

In 1993 the City of Baltimore held a competition for a master plan for its Inner Harbor, the edge of its large working harbor closest to downtown. The northernmost shoreline accommodates Harborplace, a successful but generic festival marketplace. The city's goal was to create a destination at the southern edge of the harbor adjacent to the Baltimore Museum of Science, and to interject the linear experience of the Harborplace promenade with several open spaces that express Baltimore and the Chesapeake Bay region. The competition brief also called for connecting the harbor edge with adjacent residential neighborhoods.

The winning competition proposes three distinct areas for the west shore. The first, directly adjacent to Harborplace, is a 250-foot-by-80-foot plaza that visually connects to Conway Street, the site's northern border. A second area is a willow grove with picnic tables. The third space, just north of the science museum, is a spiral fountain designed to draw people to the harbor's edge. The wooden spiral, set among a planting of native coastal grasses, descends down into the marsh and resolves into an interactive mist fountain.

The west edge of the park is created by a wide covered walkway, designed to recall waterfront warehouses and mediate between the scale of the harbor promenade and the multistory hotels and office buildings at the harbor's western shore.

The southern portion of the harbor area is a transitional zone between the bustle of the festival marketplace and the adjacent residential neighborhood of Federal Hill. A grassy bermed landform, shaped like a blue crab, symbolizes the Chesapeake in a communal front lawn for residents of adjacent neighborhoods.

The first phase construction will include the Conway Street Plaza, defined by curvy, 50-foot-tall stainless steel poles topped by fiber-optic wands that glow at night. A second plaza, adjacent to a new visitors' center, is composed of randomly arranged marble elements that recall the stoops of Baltimore rowhouses and provide seating.

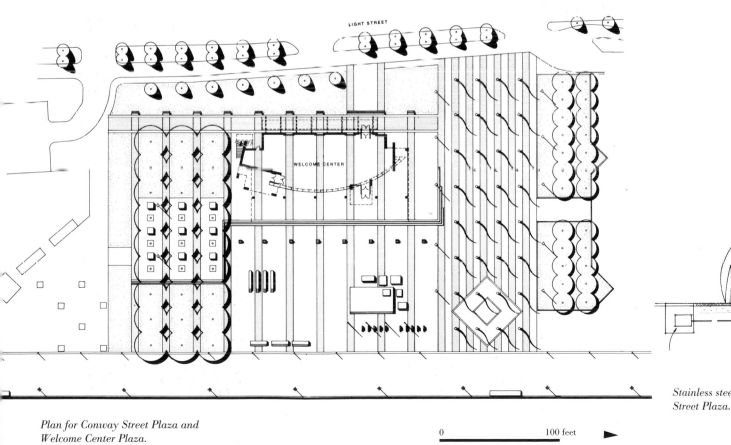

Plan for Conway Street Plaza and Welcome Center Plaza.

0   100 feet ▶

Stainless steel wand at Conway Street Plaza.

0   5 feet

Landschaftspark
München – Riem

Location: *Munich, Germany*
Client: *City of Munich*
Date: *1995*
Team: *Martha Schwartz, Inc.*
               Paula Meijerink
               Kevin Conger
               Kaki Martin
Translation: *Markus Jatsch*

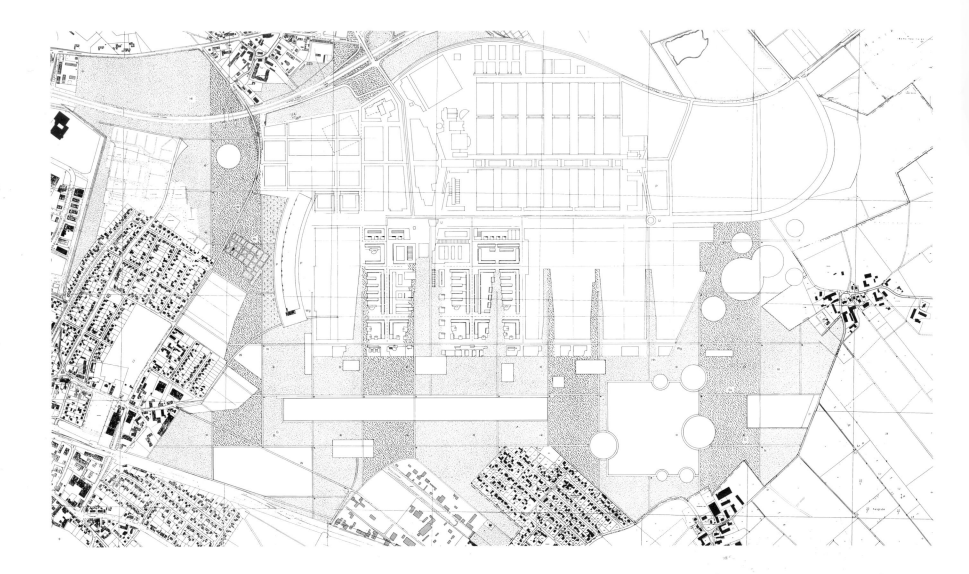

0   500 meters

*Competition entry: plan at
ground level.*

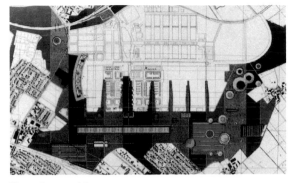

Plan of competition entry.

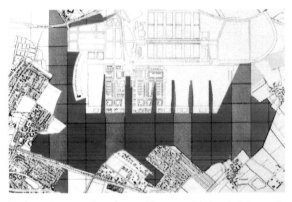

Early spring year 1 and year 10, every third strip is burned.

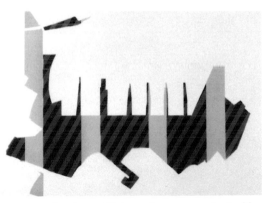

Summer year 1 and year 10, burned areas are colonized by pioneer species, remaining site is in full bloom.

Summer year 3 and year 13, entire site is in bloom.

The brief for this international competition called for a diverse natural landscape for a 518-acre park on the outskirts of Munich. However, the projected number of visitors contradicted the prescribed natural condition, which could only thrive without people.

Schwartz's proposal, which was awarded honorable mention, suggests a rigorous separation of nature and program. The flat site is interpreted as a heath, artificially maintained by grazing animals and periodic burning. To minimize human intervention upon the plane of nature, all centers of human activity appear as garden "holes." These perforations include a cemetery, child care center, athletic fields, lake, and dense forest with grottoes and rocks intended to recall the Black Forest or the Hansel and Gretel story. The design also incorporates a layer of infrastructure including roadways for emergency vehicles, call boxes and lights for safety, and garden hookups—electricity, water, and dumpsters—to encourage community gardeners.

Miami International Airport
Sound Wall

Location: Miami, FL
Client: Metro-Dade Art in
                Public Spaces
Date: 1996
Artist: Martha Schwartz
Team: Kevin Conger
                Sara Fairchild
                Chris Macfarlane
                Laura Rutledge
                Maria Bellalta
                Leo Jew
Architect: HNTB in association
                with Delante/HJ Ross
Photography: Martha Schwartz

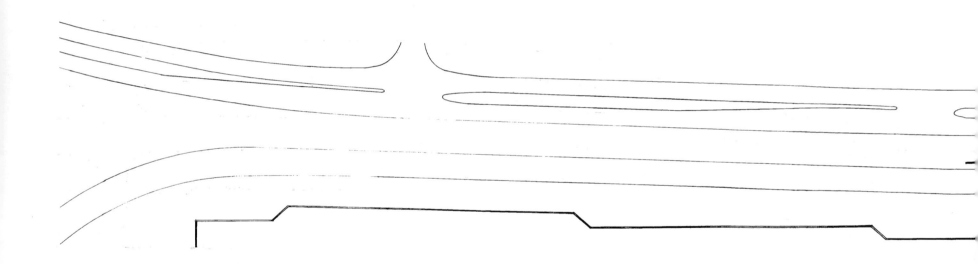

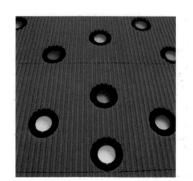

Undulating wall with undulating landscape.

Double-sided glass plugs inserted into holes in panels.

Corrugated surface of panels was a preexisting condition.

A 5-inch, smooth, black circle surrounds each hole, making colors of glass more vivid.

Colored glass and sunlight enliven a mile-long sound barrier along 36th Street, the northern boundary of the Miami International Airport. Separating the airport from two adjacent neighborhoods, the barrier is a precast concrete panel wall that ranges in height from 20 to 35 feet. The task was to make the concrete barrier wall, which the neighborhoods didn't want but the airport deemed necessary, into something the neighbors could enjoy.

Because the wall faces north, the facade along 36th Street is always cast in shadow. For this reason, solutions such as painting or appliquéing the wall with a bas-relief were rejected. "The idea behind our intervention was to use the sun to energize the wall," Schwartz explains. Holes, inset with colored glass,

are punched between the steel reinforcing bars of the wall, allowing the sun to create circles of colored light. Six different panels were designed to create the appearance of a random pattern. By scalloping the top of the wall and regrading the apron of landscape at its base, Schwartz makes the barrier appear to undulate down the mile-long stretch of roadway. At the entrance to the airport, the holes organize into a grid; the change in pattern makes the holes appear to pulsate, implying motion.

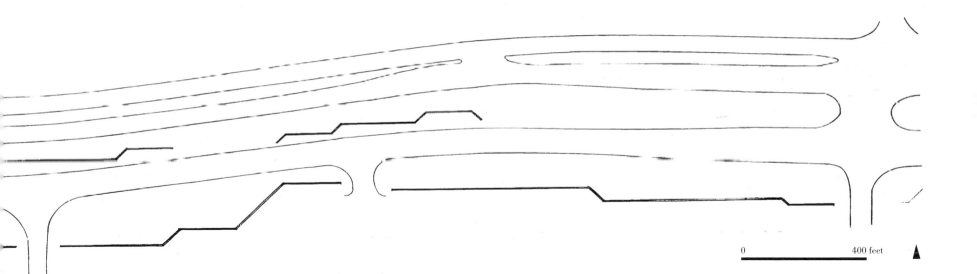

Landscape moves along with wall, minimizing awkward transitions.

Illuminated from behind by sun, colored glass plugs energize north-facing wall.

Random pattern of holes organizes into regular geometry at all airport entries.

At regular intervals, the random hole pattern intensifies and deintensifies, creating a pulsing sensation.

Notes

1 Comment made by Martha Schwartz during April 1995 Myles Thaler Memorial Lecture at the University of Virginia School of Architecture, Charlottesville, Virginia.

2 Arthur C. Danto, *The Transfiguration of the Commonplace: A Philosophy of Art* (1981), p. 208.

3 J. B. Jackson, "The Word Itself," in *Discovering the Vernacular Landscape* (1984), pp. 1-8.

4 Ibid, p. 8.

5 Denis Cosgrove and Stephen Daniels, "Introduction: Iconography and Landscape," in *The Iconography of Landscape* (1988), p. 1.

6 Danto, p. 95.

7 Danto, p. 98.

8 Martha Schwartz, Inc., project descriptions, 1995, p. 37.

9 "The belief in the Great Divide, with its aesthetic, moral, and political implications, is still dominant in the academy today. . . . But it is increasingly challenged by recent developments in the arts, literature, architecture, and criticism. This second major challenge in this century to the canonized high/low dichotomy goes by the name of postmodernism; and like the historical avantgarde though in very different ways, postmodernism rejects the theories and practices of the Great Divide. . . . The boundaries between high art and mass culture have become increasingly blurred, and we should begin to see that process as one of opportunity rather than lamenting loss of quality and failure of nerve," Andreas Huyssen, *After the Great Divide* (1986), pp. viii-ix.

10 While a graduate student at the University of Virginia, Sigrid Cook developed this line of inquiry in an excellent paper about Schwartz's work. That essay was selected for publication in *Critiques of Built Work* (1995).

11 This fountain iconography is recounted in many histories of Versailles including Hamilton Hazelhurst's *Gardens of Illusion* and Jacques Girard's *Versailles Gardens: Sculpture and Mythology*.

12 Danto, p. 208.

13 Danto, p. 208.

Bibliography

Cosgrove, Denis and Stephen Daniels. *The Iconography of Landscape.* New York: Cambridge University Press, 1988.

Danto, Arthur C. *The Transfiguration of the Commonplace: A Philosophy of Art.* Cambridge, MA: Harvard University Press, 1981.

Huyssen, Andreas. *After the Great Divide: Modernism, Mass Culture, and Postmodernism.* Bloomington: Indiana University Press, 1986.

Jackson, J. B. *Discovering the Vernacular Landscape.* New Haven: Yale University Press, 1984.

Martha Schwartz, Inc., project descriptions, 1995.

Van Valkenburgh, Michael. *Transforming the American Garden: 12 New Landscape Designs.* Cambridge, MA: Harvard University Graduate School of Design, 1986.

Photo Credits

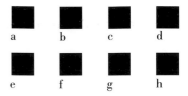

a   b   c   d

e   f   g   h

Translations

Fotografía: "Transfiguración del Lugar Comun"

Elizabeth K. Meyer

Elizabeth K. Meyer es Arquitecta Paisajista y Profesora Asociada en la Universidad de Virginia, donde dirige el Departamento de Posgrado en Arquitectura Paisajista. Enseña Talleres de Diseño y un curso sobre Arquitectura Moderna Paisajista: práctica y teoría. Antes de ser Profesora en Virginia, Meyer pertenecía al profesorado de la Universidad de Harvard y ejerció con las siguientes empresas de Arquitectura Paisajista: Michael Vergason y Asociados, Hanna/Olin y EDAW Alexandria.

The Bagel Garden, Back Bay, Boston, Massachusetts

"Un pequeño parterre está asentado dentro de setos verdes que ya existían. Hay dos rectángulos concéntricos italianizados de arbustos de boj de 40 centímetros de alto. Entre el rectángulo interior y el exterior, hay una franja de grava morada de 76 centímetros de ancho, sobre la cual descansa una serie de bagels (pan) tratados con una laca especial y colocados simétricamente. Dentro del rectángulo interior del seto, están plantados 30 agératos morados en filas de seis, revirtiendo el patrón de color morado."

–Martha Schwartz, descripción del proyecto.

The Bulb Garden de la Ciudad de Nueva York

"Esta superficie para plantío primero se llenará con 5 cm. de grava para drenaje, 30 cm. de mezcla de tierra ligera y será cubierta con 10 cm. de arena. Se colocarán 4,712 macetas de barro de 15 cm.; cada una de ellas dará cabida a una de cuatro diferentes especies de bulbos. Estas macetas se colocarán en el área de sembrado de acuerdo con un esquema de plantación para cada especie. Sus floraciones en secuencia denotan las palabras "avaricia," "maldad," "ignorancia" y "felicidad" un comentario sobre la vida urbana contemporánea. Con el fin de colocar los bulbos adecuadamente, cada maceta y bulbo tienen un número específico que los coloca dentro de una cuadrilla numerada. Los bulbos seleccionados para este diseño son narcisos, anémona griega, lirio peruano y amarilis. Estos florecen, respectivamente, en primavera, verano, principios y fines de otoño. Se seleccionaron estos bulbos por su mínima necesidad de mantenimiento y su capacidad para soportar heladas y temperaturas muy frías. Se puede regar el jardín con una manguera casera.

–Martha Schwartz, en Transformando el jardín norteamericano (1986)

Las obras de paisaje creadas por Martha Schwartz son montajes de objetos cotidianos y materiales tales como los que se pueden encontrar en los catálogos de la mayoría de las ferreterías y de las tiendas de jardinería —macetas de barro, grava de color, plantas de plástico, césped artificial (Astroturf), ornamentos de jardín (globos reflectores y ranas doradas), pintura amarillo brillante del tono de los letreros de "No estacionarse", polvo de cal, cordel y cinta. Aunque algunos de estos materiales comunes o accesorios, no son los elementos de la arquitectura paisajista que pretendan ser serios o permanentes, Schwartz expresa sus obras a través de esa disciplina. Mediante la descripción de sus proyectos, uno descubre las herramientas formales y de espacio de una diseñadora de jardines —un pequeño parterre, alamedas, setos vivos, bosquecillos, terraplen de tierra y terrazas. Es precisamente su inclusión de los lugares comunes y de lo profano; de lo disponible y de lo temporal; dentro de los límites de la arquitectura paisajista, lo que explica el enojo expresado por los miembros de la profesión cada vez que se publica un nuevo proyecto. Las obras de Schwartz, especialmente aquellas de la década de los años ochenta, fueron interpretadas como transgresiones a lo que era adecuado para la arquitectura paisajista y, aún peor, como comentarios irónicos sobre el estado de la disciplina. Los críticos tenían razón en ambos aspectos. Su obra era una forma de crear crítica y construcciones, desafiando simultáneamente las normas existentes e imaginando mundos con paisajes nuevos que sustituyeran a los viejos.

Sin embargo, Schwartz estaba perpleja y continúa estándolo por la alharaca que rodea sus obras. Después de todo, a fines de la década de los años setenta y principios de la de 1980, los artistas estaban comprometidos con actividades mucho más desafiantes que laquear ocho docenas de bagels y acomodarlos en un campo de grava de peceras, en su propio jardín delantero. "En ese momento, el artista Chris Burden se estaba crucificando para llegar a las capotas de Volkswagens, y Vito Acconci se masturbaba detrás de las escaleras, así que lo mío no me pareció nada del otro mundo," comentó Schwartz durante una conferencia en 1995.[1] Ella interpretó ésta intensa reacción hacia sus primeras obras como un síntoma de una profesión "sonámbula," un grupo de practicantes indecisos a llamar la atención hacia sus obras y hacia ellos mismos. Esta era una práctica de diseño que creaba lugares que encajan —ecológica o contextualmente— donde son más visibles, pero que generalmente retroceden a antecedentes invisibles. El recibimiento de Schwartz de parte de la profesión, se explica parcialmente por esta actitud mental en particular. Pero es igualmente sintomático de una profesión que transgrede los límites de una disciplina o, con mayor exactitud, que ocupa el territorio conceptual entre dos disciplinas, en este caso, arte contemporáneo y arquitectura del paisajista. El acto de transgresión de Schwartz, amenaza la integridad y la autonomía de una disciplina, irrita a aquellos que necesitan límites claros y viola la lógica interna de un campo.

¿Entonces por qué un artista o un diseñador desearía hacer esto? La respuesta, explícita en las obras realizadas por Schwartz, es obvia. Tales tácticas de transgresión convierten lo conocido en desconocido: en los términos del filósofo y crítico de arte, Arthur Danto, éstas "transfiguran el lugar común." Nos sacan de un estado de distracción y provocan que estemos alertas, que estemos vivos y que nos demos cuenta del mundo que nos rodea. Para un miembro de una disciplina cuyos linderos están copados por dicha transfiguración, esta sacudida perceptual está acompañada de tal revelación intelectual, que los formalismos de la disciplina, que previamente habían sido tomados como "un hecho," no solamente se han cuestionado, sino que han sido clarificados—vistos realmente—por primera vez. Danto explica este fenómeno en una discusión sobre el uso que hace Andy Warhol de objetos comunes:

> ...esta transfiguración de un objeto común, no transforma nada en el mundo del arte. Sólo trae a la conciencia las estructuras del arte que, para mayor seguridad, necesitaron un cierto desarrollo histórico antes de que la metáfora fuese posible. En el momento que fue posible, algo como la caja "brillo" fue inevitable y sin sentido. Fue inevitable porque la acción tenía que llevarse a cabo, ya fuera con éste o con cualquier otro objeto.[2]

Desde esta perspectiva, los proyectos de Martha Schwartz obran como una especie de esfera de análisis o de mirada reflectora dentro de la profesión. Estos señalan un lugar específico, pero implican mayores espacios y a otros diseñadores. Vemos que nuestro trabajo, nuestros valores y nuestras hipótesis se renuevan cada vez que Schwartz transfigura un lugar común con materiales comunes.

¿Qué significa desafiar los límites del paisaje?

¿Por qué la obra de Schwartz es tan provocativa? Una razón es el grado hasta el cual desafía, no solamente la disciplina de la arquitectura paisajista, sino también la definición de paisaje. Ahora estamos conscientes de que paisaje es una palabra dúctil. Los principales escritos de J. B. Jackson, particularmente "La palabra en sí misma,"[3] rastrea la evolución del significado de paisaje. El ofrece una nueva definición que proporciona un marco incómodo para las obras de Schwartz:

> ...una composición de espacios hechos o modificados por el hombre para servir de infraestructura o antecedentes de nuestra existencia colectiva; y si "antecedentes" parece demasiado modesta, debemos recordar que en su acepción moderna, la palabra significa aquello que subraya no sólo nuestra identidad y presencia, sino también nuestra historia.[4]

La mayoría de los paisajes de Schwartz, tales como los del Centro Comercial de Río y la Plaza de Housing and Urban Development, con su claridad visual y asertividad, son todo menos "antecedentes." Quizá son escenarios para la acción, pero no antecedentes mudos. Además, Jackson narra que los norteamericanos tienen una tendencia a considerar paisaje como sinónimo de escenario natural, pintorescas imágenes bucólicas o selváticas. Como sociedad, nosotros nos imaginamos el paisaje como algo dado; no a muchos se nos ocurre que las escenas rurales que tanto valoramos son construcciones humanas: son formadas, modeladas y cuidadas. Al contrario de los ingleses, nosotros pensamos en el paisaje como algo natural, no construido.

Las obras de Schwartz, hechas con materiales sintéticos disponibles, ordenados a través de atrevidas figuras y geometrías de repetición o en serie y realizadas con un toque de ingenio, son construcciones culturales conscientes. Desafían las categorías de pensamiento que estructuran la definición de paisaje establecida por la profesión y por la cultura popular. Natural contra cultural; duradero contra temporal; real contra sintético; serio contra irónico y antecedentes contra futuro. Este reto a la definición de paisaje, da mayor relevancia a la arquitectura paisajista. No bastándoles con formar antecedentes para la vida y el arte, sino aspirando a representar la vida y el arte a través del paisaje, las obras de Schwartz resuenan con una idea de paisaje propuesta por dos geógrafos ingleses, Denis Cosgrove y Stephen Daniels. Ellos escriben:

> El paisaje es una imagen cultural, una manera pictórica de representar, estructurar o simbolizar el entorno. Esto no quiere decir que los paisajes sean incorpóreos, pueden representarse en diversos materiales y sobre muchas superficies -en pintura sobre un lienzo, en escritura sobre un papel, en tierra, en piedra, en agua y sobre vegetación en el suelo.[5]

Los proyectos de Schwartz llevados a cabo, exigen que el paisaje no sólo realice la función de acomodar. Los espacios y las formas del paisaje, también deben representar, englobar y simbolizar cómo ve uno el mundo.

Desafíos a las prácticas de paisaje de fines del siglo XX.
Danto sugiere que la serie de cajones "brillo" de Warhol, aclaran las estructuras normativas a través de las cuales, se definió y se criticó el arte en la década de los años sesenta. Los paisajes populares de Schwartz tienen el mismo efecto. Iluminan las estructuras y las críticas a través de las cuales los arquitectos paisajistas definen los tipos de proyectos que conciben, los tipos de lugares dignos de su atención y los principios de diseño que utilizan. ¿Cuáles son los desafíos para estos supuestos estructurales? El primero es fundamental —que los arquitectos paisajistas están comprometidos con una práctica que está enrredada tanto en lo cultural como en lo natural; tanto en lo artificial como en lo real. Los humanos viven imaginando el mundo a través de un lente cultural; valoramos los paisajes, la naturaleza y lo salvaje debido a su rol en nuestra cultura. En otras palabras, generalmente no estamos trabajando con alguna versión de una naturaleza inmaculada e incorrupta. El segundo dasafío se refiere a la ceguera que padecen muchos arquitectos paisajistas en cuanto a la penetración de paisajes vernáculos, suburbanos e industriales, y como estos espacios a los que se ha dado forma pueden proporcionar material e inspiración para un diseñador. En vez de alejarse de estos paisajes de asfalto, de desarrollo especulativo, de construcción barata y de gusto cuestionable, uno puede reconocer su influencia en la cultura popular. Proyectos como el de Centro de Convenciones Columbus y el Centro para Tecnología Innovadora, abarcan los tipos espaciales y materiales reales de los paisajes encontrados en las colonias periféricas, en las franjas estrechas de terreno y en los estacionamientos.

El tercer desafío para la profesión se relaciona con el segundo. Existe una tendencia a limitar el alcance de la arquitectura paisajista a espacios que merecen el esfuerzo: parques urbanos, plazas y sedes corporativas, jardines hermosos, campos universitarios, y demas. Uno no debería desperdiciar energías en espacios menos prestigiados: el estacionamiento, franjas estrechas de terreno en líneas divisorias, carreteras secundarias, el espacio remanente entre edificios, zonas marginales dentro de los edificios. Esas áreas son abandonadas o descuidadas, tanto por sus propietarios como por muchos arquitectos paisajistas. Por consiguiente, su caracter es la consecuencia involuntaria de otras decisiones del resultado de la intervención de un ingeniero. Schwartz ve estos espacios no sólo como importantes, sino como vitales para la profesión, dado el pequeño número de proyectos en sitios prestigiosos y lo ubicuo de los demas. Los proyectos de Citadel, del Instituto Whitehead y del Aeropuerto Internacional de Miami, sacan provecho de espacios invisibles o de poca importancia, y al hacer esto, ayudan a crear lugares de territorios que de otra manera serian alienantes.

Finalmente, la gama de materiales de Schwartz, no evoca ni espacios de naturaleza ni de gusto refinado. En lugar de una larga lista de árboles, arbustos, plantas, superficies de granito térmico y pasamanos tallados a mano, uno encuentra concreto de color estampado, concreto con aspecto de piedra, asfalto, pintura de uso general, unidades de mampostería, fibra de vidrio, césped artificial, acrílico plexiglass, barreras de tráfico, vías y señales de ferrocarril, llantas y otros artículos confeccionados facilmente. Esta falta de refinamiento, esta inclusión de materiales comunes (facilmente disponibles y vulgares), ofende a algunos que asocian estos artículos con jardines de mal gusto de las colonias periféricas, o con espacios industriales. Schwartz reacciona con un argumento respecto a que estos son los materiales disponibles y no caros de la industria de la construcción. ¿Por qué no intentar hacer algo

honesto y hermoso con ellos? ¿Por qué no intentar transfigurar el lugar común? El pragmatismo y el populismo de este enfoque, frecuentemente se ve obscurecido por debates sobre estilo y belleza. Si Danto esta correcto en su opinion en cuanto a que la belleza "puede no tener un valor descriptivo,"[6] pero que puede estar codificada en la relación de uno con el mundo y puede ser una "función de lo que creemos con respecto a un objeto,"[7] entonces quizas podamos atender a las razones por las que no valoramos estos materiales y artículos. Estos prejuicios y parcialidades pueden estar limitando nuestra habilidad para crear mundos paisajistas nuevos o para imaginar nuevas formas de la belleza.

La practica de Schwartz, además de presentar desafíos a la disciplina y a la profesión de la arquitectura paisajista, también confronta la profesión de la arquitectura y su marginalización de paisaje como un sujeto y un espacio. Actualmente se está poniendo a pruba este desafío retórico a través del rediseño de tres plazas relacionadas con ejemplos de la arquitectura moderna tardía, la Corte Federal en Minneapolis, las oficinas del Departamento de Vivienda y Desarrollo Urbano (HUD) de los Estados Unidos, en Washington, D.C., realizado por Marcel Breuer y el Edificio Federal Jacob Javits en la ciudad de Nueva York, donde hasta recientemente, estaba ubicado el "Tilted Arc" de Richard Serra. Estas propuestas específicas son críticas construidas de la represión del paisaje por parte de la arquitectura moderna y su confinación del paisaje a un espacio abierto, a una tabula rasa; un podio para un edificio de un objeto escultural. En lugar de este pobre rol, Schwartz presenta a la arquitectura con un nuevo conjunto de convenciones para el paisaje. Estas incluyen el reconocimiento de que vivimos en el espacio, tanto interior como exterior, y que el diseño no puede terminar en el muro del edificio; que un edificio es sólo un objeto en medio de una naturaleza muerta conformada por muchos objetos; que el paisaje, así como la arquitectura, no solamente tiene forma, sino contenido y que el espacio está lleno, no abierto, antes que una arquitectura es llamada a la acción. Schwartz es tan agresiva en la reconstrucción de estos difíciles espacios urbanos, como los arquitectos que la precedieron. En Washington, D.C., la sede central del HUD, diseñadas por Breuer en la década de los años sesenta, personifican las sensibilidades urbanas de ese periodo. Este edificio de concreto en forma de X está elevado sobre pilotis, en el centro de una parcela no articulada de seis acres. La propuesta de Schwartz, llama a no sólo reafirmar la esfera pública mediante una alfombra tridimensional de lechos circulares para plantío y paredes de asientos cubiertos de coloridos discos de vinilo para crear sombra, sino que también sugiere demoler parte de la planta baja del edificio para crear conexiones entre los cuatro cuadrantes de la parcela no relacionados entre sí. En la ciudad de Nueva York, donde el diseño paisajista urbano contemporáneo puede reducirse a seleccionar artículos en existencia de la lista de materiales apropiados del Departamento de Parques, tales como bancas de la Feria de las Naciones, de los estandares de iluminacion de Central Park, cercos de hierro fundido, bancas de granito y pavimentos de piedra azul, Schwartz está adoptando otra estrategia para objetivar la esfera pública. Siguiendo las reglas del juego, la propuesta de diseño de Schwartz para la plaza Jacob Javitz incluye, en sus propias palabras, "elementos tradicionales de parque de Nueva York con un rasgo humorístico."[8] Estos elementos están transfigurados, no solamente a través de sus distorsiones dimensionales, (los estandares de iluminacion se atenúan a partir de 365 a 914 cm. de altura) sino también a través de su montaje y alineación. Por ejemplo, las bancas comunes de tablillas de madera, están alineadas en grandes curvas invertidas que crean un diseño similar al *embroiderie* de espirales y nudos, dentro del parterre de un jardín francés. Mediante su hibridación del mobiliario de parques y de sus planos de jardín, Schwartz introduce Gilmore Clarke a André Le Notre. El resultado es un diseño que habla de su propio tiempo mientras cita de su pasado, sin recurrir al contextualismo genérico de tantos otros paisajes públicos recientes en la ciudad de Nueva York. Un último ejemplo de esta postura agresiva hacia un espacio arquitectónico preexistente, es su proclividad a trabajar tanto la superficie vertical como la horizontal. Tanto el Jardín Turf Parterre, instalado temporalmente en Battery Park City, asi como el Whitehead Institute Splice Garden en Cambridge, Massachusetts, siguen diseños y gestos desde el suelo hacia el muro, de lo horizontal a lo vertical, transgrediendo los límites de construcción y de alcance que se consideran apropiados para un arquitecto paisajista.

La obra de Martha Schwartz a medida que demuestra una práctica posmoderna.
Esta tendencia a desafiar los límites conceptuales de una disciplina, es una característica de muchas prácticas culturales en las últimas décadas del siglo XX. Desde este punto de vista, Schwartz es una posmodernista típica. Ha encontrado momentos para invencion en los bordes o márgenes de dos campos, en intersección del arte público y de la arquitectura paisajista. Además, al desdoblar irónicamente en sus obras imágenes y materiales de la cultura de masas,

Schwartz ha desafiado lo que el crítico cultural Andreas Huyssen llamó la "gran linea divisoria" entre el arte elitista y la cultura de masas y, al hacer esto, consolida su posición como una posmodernista.[9] Sin embargo, Schwartz se sitúa a sí misma y a su obra, dentro de un marco moderno. Un análisis formal de sus obras confirma esto. Espacios geométricos puros y figuras tales como cuadrados, círculos y elipses, flotan por encima de campos hechos tensos por diseños rítmicos repetitivos. Cuadrículas estiradas por su extension tridimensional, cajas, son animadas por su yuxtaposición con objetos de gran escala. Los mecanismos de ordenamiento del arte abstracto y del arte minimalista son apropiadas y aplicadas a la esfera del paisaje. Huyssen opina que es esta utilización de mecanismos formales modernos a un nuevo contexto, dentro de un nuevo campo conceptual que incluye aquello que anteriormente se excluía, es la clave de la práctica posmoderna. Las obras de Schwartz incluyen la continuación de lo moderno como una crítica del mismo; tanto la materializacion de los principios formales del arte moderno y el uso irreverente de aquellas estrategias en un nuevo campo. Esta perspectiva teórica, nos permite ver a Schwartz como algo más que una renegada desertora en la profesión de arquitectura paisajista; la redefine a ella y a obras de arquitectura paisajista, como participantes activos en una esfera creativa y cultural más amplia, y define la arquitectura paisajista asi como tambien una práctica cultural así como una profesión.

Esta lectura de Schwartz como una practicante cultural posmoderna, que busca fortalecer lo moderno a través de la contaminación y la reinscripcion, ofrece una alternativa a la modalidad conservadora de la práctica posmoderna que rechaza la modernidad y substituye una modalidad de historicismo o contextualismo. De la misma manera que espíritus afines en arte y arquitectura, tales como Warhol y Robert Venturi o Rem Koolhaas, Schwartz ha tomado en cuenta el mercado comercial, la cultura de masas, las franjas estrechas de terreno y las colonias periféricas, como fuentes de contenido y contaminación. Ella ha incluido esas influencias dentro de un nuevo campo: el arte y la práctica de jardines y paisajes. En eso estriba su singularidad.

Martha Schwartz, como participe o externa

A pesar de estos lazos con prácticas de arte contemporáneo, con campos dentro de la profesión de arquitectura y con prácticas culturales posmodernas más amplias, Martha Schwartz tiene pocas almas gemelas en la arquitectura paisajista contemporánea. Sin embargo, a pesar de esta inmersión en los discursos teoricos de otros campos, las obras de Schwartz se identifican con las tradiciones de la arquitectura paisajista y con el oficio de hacer jardines. Debido a que las partes que ella reune para construir sus fantasías son parterres, arbustos recortados artisticamente y bosques: la obra confronta. Debido a las asociaciones de las formas de sus paisajes con ornamentos vernáculos y de alta jardinería: la obra ofende. De hecho, lo que da fuerza a la obra de Schwartz, es la intensa relación con la historia y con las tradiciones de la arquitectura paisajista y del arte. De otra manera, ella sería simplemente una artista más ampliando su ambito hacia un nuevo campo, pero olvidándose de sus tradiciones —otra Mary Miss o Elyn Zimmerman. En lugar de esto, las referencias explícitas de Schwartz a las tradiciones de hacer jardin, la colocan firmemente, tanto dentro del arte y dentro del diseño paisajista, como en la intersección entre ambos.

¿Cuáles son estos lazos con las tradiciones de la arquitectura paisajista? Desde luego, existe la extracción y distorsión de partes del jardin frances del siglo XVII, en proyectos como el Bagel Garden, el Necco Garden, el Whitehead Institute Splice Garden y el King County Jailhouse Garden. Estas secciones, *embroiderie* y parterres, pueden ser descritos de una manera tan creible como lo hace Antoine-Joseph d'Argenville Dezallier en su tratado, *La Théorie et la Practique du Jardinage* (1709), así como también por un artista de fines del siglo XX.[10] Este tratado jardin frances, describe las prácticas de diseñar un parterre, plasmándolo en papel con instrumentos utilizados de dibujo, y transfiriendo luego ese diseño al terreno con estacas y cordel, técnicas evocadas en documentacion fotográfica de la instalación temporal del Necco Garden en las inmediaciones del MIT. La invencion que se asocia con estas citas históricas autoconscientes, gira alrededor de la representacion de estas formas con materiales inesperados -plástico, neumaticos, dulces y trabajo de azulelos ceramicos rotos. Haciendo lo conocido, desconocido. Transfigurando el lugar común.

En ocasiones, las formas de un jardín evocan asociaciones que desconciertan tanto al propietario, como al crítico. ¿Qué debemos deducir de las ranas doradas que contemplan el globo con malla de alambre del Centro Comercial de Río? Tal vez sean los ornamentos de jardín más baratos disponibles en los suburbios de Atlanta, pero, dada su ubicación en una fuente de agua y su radiante relación con la orbe dominante, uno se ve tentado a compararla con la Fuente Latona en Versaille, donde un grupo de ranas boquiabiertas se posan en albardillas concéntricas de piedra. La estatua central, elevada por sobre las fuentes circulares y las ranas, es de los hijos de Latona y Júpiter, Diana y Apolo, el futuro "rey sol."[11] De acuerdo con el mito, las ranas en realidad son campesinos a quienes el dios Júpiter transformo en anfibios inferiores debido a su irrespetuosa mofa de los hijos de Latona y Júpiter. ¿Quién ha estado mofandose de Schwartz y por qué están condenados de por vida a adorar el globo de kudzú? O, ¿de quién se está mofando Schwartz? ¿De los críticos que dicen que esto no es arquitectura paisajista y quienes no conocen su propia historia lo suficientemente bien como para apreciar una buena broma de jardín cuando la ven?

Otros aspectos de la obra de Schwartz, tales como sus terrazas-jardin, la relacionan con diseñadores de principios del siglo XX como Guevrekian y Le Corbusier. Particularmente, el surrealismo y la objetivización de la naturaleza en el Splice Garden, evocan experimentos de diseño de jardines de las décadas de los años veinte y treinta. La terraza-jardín de Guevrekian en la Villa Noailles en Hyeres, Francia, fue un modelo a seguir para los arquitectos paisajistas pertenecientes al modernismo temprano. La publicación de Fletcher Steele en la prensa norteamericana acerca ese jardín, sacudio a la profesión fuera de su complacencia en las Bellas Artes. Además de compartir su papel detonador con las terrazas-jardin de Schwartz, el jardín Guevrekian, también explora la relación entre el ordenamiento perceptual y el conceptual en su distorsión del plano de tierra y su estructura perceptual asociada. El resultado es una superficie que oscila entre la horizontal y la vertical, que requiere del que visita el jardín entanblarse en un juego óptico y perceptual. Esta táctica se aplica en el Splice Garden, donde, tanto la superficie de césped artificial y los arbustos recortados artisticamente, saltan de piso a pared y a cornisa. Este aspecto surrealista del Splice Garden, en el que las formas adoptan dimensiones exageradas y ubicaciones extrañas, se asemeja mucho al juego que se encuentra en una de las terrazas-jardin Beistegui de Le Corbusier, en París.

La tercera referencia para contextualizar la obra de Schwartz dentro de las tradiciones del hacer de jardines y paisajes, atienen a su tendencia reciente de representar el plano de tierra a través de dar forma escultural a la tierra. Mientras que es tentador mencionar a Noguchi, Smithson y Heizer como precursores, uno no deberia ignorar las tradiciones de la construcción de monticulos Japoneses, las exploraciones contemporáneas de James Rose, Garrett Eckbo y A. E. Bye, como investigaciones relacionadas. Los esculturales y enfáticos movimientos de los espacios de Schwartz, son mucho más poderosos debido a su ubicación sobre superficies consideradas invisibles por la arquitectura contemporánea. La plaza del Palacio de Justicia de Minneapolis, está pensada en relacion a su escala y representada con un enjambre de monticulos de cilindros elípticos que establecen tanto una dirección de movimiento como un instrumento secundario de ajuste para la plaza. En el trabajo conjunto de Schwartz con Rem Koolhaas, en el Kunsthal Museumpark en Rotterdam, ella representa el plano horizontal como un monticulo elíptico negro brilloso emergiendo de una gran fuente de agua. Alli, el interés de Koolhaas en el uso de escalas y en la yuxtaposición de escalas dentro del medio ambiente urbano contemporáneo, está acompañado por la presencia asertiva de un paisaje escultural. En el World Trade Towers Plaza, depresiones circulares reconocen la imposibilidad de hacer un objeto u objetos de paisaje para sostener a estos gigantes. Así, la palnta se articula en cortes muy sutiles —una serie de platos cóncavos esculpidos dentro de la superficie de la plaza, imperceptibles, excepto cuando se llenan de agua. Entonces ellos constituyen un campo de piletas uniformemente distribuidas a través de la plaza.

Dos proyectos extienden esta representación del plano de tierra a la dimensión simbólica. El más reciente, el West Shore and Rash Field Park en Baltimore, incluye un onduloso campo de césped intersectada con senderos estrechos. Cuando se ve como una serie, los monticulos individuales se congelan con la forma de un cangrejo azul, un manjar por el que son famosos Baltimore y Chesapeake Bay. En el límite de lo "kitsch", este cangrejo de tierra alude a la cultura local, una imagen popularmente asociada con la región. Destinado a convertirse en un chiste local, conocido por la comunidad y señalado desde ventanas de aviones cuando uno vuela sobre la el Inner Harbor, el cangrejo azul se las ingenio para hacer un lugar, para rescatar el paisaje de una condición de invisibilidad y espacio abierto. Menos ingenioso pero igualmente alusivo, es el extendido terraplen en forma de una larga barra que propuso Schwartz para el Holocaust Memorial Competition en Boston. Este terraplen, hecho de un bloque de concreto de 106.7 metros de largo por 3.65 metros de alto, es, al mismo tiempo, hecho de la tierra. Esta forma de masa parece surgir del mismo suelo, un medio estrecho, asaltado por autos y turistas. Sin embargo, la entereza del Monumento es negada por su construccion hecha con unidades pequeñas, miles de ellas. Simultáneamente, es un terraplen mortuorio etrusco y horno de un campo de concentración; un lugar de descanso y demalestar; cementerio y crematorio. Es una cosa, es una multiplicidad de singularidades. Es un sitio de horror, una versión posmoderna de lo sublime. El proyecto resuena con significados, propuestos debido a las imágenes que no son conocidas de la cultura de masas, así como también, las formas y tipologías que conocemos a través de la historia del paisaje.

La fuerza de los paisajes tanto especulativos como construidos de Martha Schwartz, es función de su naturaleza híbrida. Sus proyectos están llenos de citas, formales e iconográficas, a las costumbres y tradiciones de la jardinería. Sin embargo, son imaginadas a través de los ojos y las manos de una artista y una consumidora de la cultura de masa, quien, percibe valor y significado en lo facilmente disponible, en lo ya elaborado y en lo que se produce en serie.

Paisajes como símbolos e imágenes

La obra de Martha Schwartz hace surgir preguntas sobre cómo y a quién comunican los paisajes. Dadas sus múltiples lealtades hacia los discursos teoricos del arte y la arquitectura paisajista; hacia la cultura de masas; así como también con el arte elitista; hacia lo permanente y lo temporal; hacia lo ingenioso y lo profundo; es sorprendente que su obra sea difícil de decifrar. Como este ensayo, ha intentado demostrar a través de algunos ejemplos, el acto de interpretación bien vale la pena el esfuerzo. Para aquellos que están dentro del campo de la arquitectura paisajista, estas obras recien ahora estan llegando a su madurez profesional, "se ofrecen a sí mismas como un espejo".[12] En esa superficie se refleja la falta de forma y la superficialidad de una gran parte de la profesión. La obra de Schwartz no trata solamente de hacer que el paisaje sea visible, lo está fortaleciendo con significado. Para aquellos en el campo de la arquitectura, las obras paisajistas de Schwartz resisten el impulso de asumir un sitio vacío, de despejar el sitio antes de diseñar. Sus proyectos requieren de arquitectos que abran sus edificios a la comunicación con sus alrededores y, más directamente, con su plano de tierra, la superficie sobre la cual se desarrolla la vida. Y para aquellos fuera de estos dos campos de diseño, la imprecisa posición desordenada de Schwartz entre el arte y la arquitectura paisajista, revela poco profundas que son muchos trabajos pretenden desdibujar los límites de una disciplina. En comparación, muchas de estas obras son una forma de colonización disciplinaria, un asentamiento en un territorio ajeno, sin conocimiento de sus tradiciones, convenciones, idiomas o costumbres. La obra de Schwartz ofrece una alternativa, una actividad híbrida que extrae significado y formas de dos corrientes de pensamiento y práctica, con la intención, ni de transformar una disciplina, ni de reorientar la otra. Adopta esta difícil posición como un medio para redefinir el papel y el significado de paisaje en una cultura de consumo.

Un proyecto diseñado por Martha Schwartz y sus colegas, no solamente desafía nuestros ojos: desafía nuestra inteligencia. Así como Danto resume la función de esas cajas "Brillo," también nosotros podemos reconsiderar aquellos paisajes de bagels, Neccos, ranas doradas, parterres de césped artificial, los faroles y bancas de la ciudad de Nueva York transformados y cangrejos de tierra. "Logra lo que las obras de arte siempre han logrado —exteriorizar una manera de ver el mundo, expresando el interior de un periodo cultural y ofreciéndose como un espejo para despertar la consciencia de nuestros reyes."[13] Para otros arquitectos paisajistas, los proyectos de Schwartz hacen rezaltar las estructuras conceptuales a través de las cuales definimos nuestra disciplina. Aclaran los límites actuales y señalan nuevas direcciones o posibilidades.

Martha Schwartz ha dicho que no todas las obras tienen que ser obras maestras -perdurables, eternas y veneradas. ¿Qué quiere decir con esto? Para ciertas obras puede ser suficiente ser vehículos para re-presentar el paisaje ante una comunidad, un cliente, un consultor. Esta idea de proposiciones de diseño como re-presentaciones, como una caja para re-ver, como un vidrio de Claude reflectivo y cóncavo, de fines del siglo XX, establece un marco para poder apreciar obras temporales, lugares comunes -sitios descuidados o marginales y materiales o cosas comunes y corrientes. Permite a otros observar el paisaje con una nueva óptica, una óptica menos enamorada de una naturaleza ideal e inalcanzable y que acepta el paisaje real en toda su fuerza descarnada. En tanto que los trabajos de Schwartz incluyen cada vez más lo permanente y lo público, uno se pregunta sobre si sería posible integrar la expresión artística, la crítica cultural, el gesto retórico con la concepción dehacer "lugar" y a la creación de una obra maestra. Las obras maestras, encargadas por los mecenas adinerados, han venido a significar hermosas composiciones realizadas con materiales perdurables pero, desgraciadamente, carentes de contenido o significado. ¿Puede una práctica dedicada a transfigurar el lugar común, mientras construye a la vista pública y en lugares marginales aspirar a la creación de obras maestras?

Martha Schwartz lleva 15 años de experimentos, montajes temporales, de pequeños trabajos por encargo y tiene mecenas leales que la apoyan. Una revisión de esta recopilacion de obras como un todo, revela el poder de una crítica cultural más sustancial que los gestos retóricos de proyectos individuales. Esta práctica de diseño como crítica cultural, y representada escultural y espacialmente en plástico, concreto prensado y partes producidas en serie, ha ofrecido a la profesión una manera de construir un mundo en el paisaje duro, de crecimiento desordenado, comercial de las franjas angostas de terreno, las carreteras y las colonias periféricas. Si existe un territorio a fines de siglo XX, que necesita urgentemente la creacion de "lugar" que el urbanismo tradicional y subcedaneo, es el límite urbano-suburbano; la esfera de lote de centro comerciales, lugares de comida al paso y corredores comerciales de grandes "cajas", y nuestros hogares, el lugar donde la mayoría de los norteamericanos viven. Ahora que este lugar común y sus problemas nos han sido descriptos, transfigurados de un lugar inexistente a un lugar adonde ir, tal vez otros seguirán la dirección de Martha Schwartz. Más que verla como una iconoclasta, como una artista ingeniosa y como una destructora de la profesión, esta crítica piensa que ya es hora de reconocer su crítica sustancial y sus contribuciones materiales, tanto al paisaje norteamericano, como a la arquitectura paisajista. (Notas en la página 160)

Reconocimientos

Durante los últimos 8 años, he podido resolver muchas de mis ideas acerca de la arquitectura contemporánea paisajista junto con mis estudiantes, primero en la Universidad de Harvard y actualmente en la Universidad de Virginia. A ellos agradezco el darme un público siempre entusiasta e inteligente. Además, la investigación hecha por estudiantes y el escribir para mi curso, han cambiado o clarificado mi comprensión de ciertos diseñadores. En particular Sigrid Cook, Kevin Rasmussen, Alison Ingram y Eric Chou, me ayudaron a apreciar con mayor profundidad los diseños de Martha Schwartz, tales como el Centro Comercial de Río de Janeiro, el Splice Garden y el CIT. Finalmente quiero agradecerle a Kaki Martin, colaborador de Martha Schwartz, por su ayuda al proporcionarme descripciones verbales y gráficas del trabajo de la firma.

Notas:

1 Comentario hecho por Martha Schwartz durante la Lectura Memorial Myles Thaler en Abril de 1995, en la Facultad de Arquitectura de la Universidad de Virginia, Charlottesville, Virginia.

2 Arthur C. Danto, *The Transfiguration of the Commonplace: A Philosophy of Art* (1981), p. 208.

3 J. B. Jackson, "The Word Itself," en *Discovering the Vernacular Landscape* (1984), pp. 1-8.

4 Ibid, p. 8.

5 Denis Cosgrove y Stephen Daniels, "Introduction: Iconography and landscape," en *The Iconography of Landscape* (1988), p. 1.

6 Danto, p. 95.

7 Danto, p. 98.

8 Martha Schwartz, Inc., descripiciones de proyectos, 1995, p. 37.

9 "Esta creencia en la Great Divide, con las implicaciones esteticas, morales y politicas, es todavia dominate en la academia hoy en día . . . Pero es constantemente desafiada por recientes desarrollos en las artes, literatura, arquitectura y el criticismo. El sugundo desafio mas grande ed este siglo tiene pornombre posmodernismo; y como el histórico vanguardista, aunque en muchas maneras diferentes, el posmodernismo rechaza las teorías y prácticas de la Great Divide . . . Los límites entre la elevada arte y la cultura masiva se han hecho cada vez mas borrosos, y nosotros deberíamos empezar a ver el proceso como una oportunidad, en vez de lamentarnos por perdida de calidad y fracaso de valor," Andreas Huyssen, *After the Great Divide* (1986), pp. viii-ix.

10 Mientras atendiendo la Universidad de Virginia como una estudiante egresada, Sigrid Cook desarrollo este tipo de investigación en una exelente redacción acerca del trabajo de Schwartz. Esa redacción fue seleccionada para publicación en *Critiques of Built Work* (1995).

11 Esta fuente de iconografía esta recontada en muchas historias de Versailles, estos incluyen *Gardens of Illusion* por Hamilton Hazelhurst, y *Versailles Gardens: Sculpture and Mythology* por Jacques Girard's.

12 Danto, p. 208.

13 Danto, p. 208.

Entrevista con Martha Schwartz

Conocida por disponer materiales facilmente disponibles o temporaneos, colores brillantes y diseños geométricos en no convencionales diseños, Martha Schwartz ocasionalmente ha sorprendido a una profesión impregnada al legado de Frederick Law Olmsted. No obstante, Schwartz ha diseñado paisajes que parecen ser más desafiantes, más irónicos e innovadores en cada obra. Aquí, ella habla de las influencias que guían su trabajo para clientes privados, de corporaciones y gubernamentales.

Usted es conocida por incorporar al paisaje materiales inusitados. ¿Puede hablarnos sobre la elección de sus materiales?

Al principio, mis materiales surgieron de mi interés en el Arte Pop. Fui atraida por la cualidad subversiva de utilizar materiales sencillos y objetos de descarte. Me atraían obras de arte como el foco de luz hecho de Jasper Johns, esa improbable expresión del lugar comun con lo preciado. La exaltación de los objetos cotidianos, era una noción anti-prevaleciente del arte que me intrigó. Me encantaban las cajas "brillo" de Andy Warhol, y su desafio al mundo del arte, respecto a lo que era considerado como "Arte."

En esa época, la mayoría de la gente opinaba que las cajas "brillo" de ninguna manera pertenecían en un museo. En mi opinión, se podía y se debía romper con las reglas dentro del establecimiento del arte. Los artistas que trabajaban con la tierra me interesaron por las mismas razones: su trabajo era conceptual y en un específico del sitio; no podía llevarse al mundo de las galerías de arte. Desde mucho antes de que supiera que existía la arquitectura paisajista, yo quería desafiar el pensamiento y las creencias convencionales.

Cuando empecé a estudiar arquitectura paisajista, me di cuenta que la profesión invierte mucho en el saber de oficio artesanal, la tradición y el uso de materiales de alta calidad. Pensé que habia demasiado valor puesto en el oficio y una falta de materiales, y que no se preocupaban o no de interes, en los aspectos conceptuales de una obra. En el arte, el concepto es central para la obra; en el paisaje, la función es lo cetral.

Pensaba que la falta de rigor en cuanto a los conceptos e ideas estaba, tal vez, relacionada con la atención centrada en los materiales y en el oficio. Quizá la arquitectura paisajista podría ir hacia adelante si fueramos alentados a pensar en los materiales de una manera más amplia. Podríamos incrementar nuestro lenguaje conceptual; los cordones de granito podían ser de plástico reciclado, vidrio, marmol o césped artificial. En el lenguaje, la falta de vocabulario limita lo que uno puede pensar. De la misma manera, la falta de posibilidades de materiales limitaba el pensamiento conceptual en la arquitectura paisajista.

Mi postura en ese momento era la de dar ascento a los materiales asociados con cultura. Ahora, sin embargo, soy la reina de los trabajos con presupuestos reducidos. Nunca he realizado un proyecto en el que haya podido especificar piedra labrada. Mis diseños son hechos con materiales que no son caros porque mis clientes no pueden permitirse el lujo de construir proyectos caros. He hecho un lugar para un mismo decir: "De acuerdo, asi que no puedes gastar 131 dólares por metro cuadrado, haremos algo con integridad y merito por 23 dólares. Usaremos cemento o asfalto colado-en-sitio, y enfocaremos esto de una manera positiva."

La cambiante realidad es que tenemos menos recursos. Ser capaz de hacer algo excepcional con materiales sencillos, ya no es una opción, es una necesidad.

Con frecuencia me preguntan por qué elijo materiales que tendrán que ser reparados o remplazados. La gente cree que nosotros los artistas y diseñadores, podemos elegir la calidad de los materiales; en realidad, es el cliente quien establece el nivel al establecer un presupuesto. Cuando se está decidiendo un proyecto, yo no estoy ahí para preguntar, "¿Realmente en cuánto valúa este paisaje? ¿Quiere que perdure 100 años o solamente una tarde?" Esos valores se reflejan a través de la cantidad de dinero que se invierte en el proyecto, un parámetro muy sencillo. Puedo tratar de pesuadir a la gente para que cambie esos valores, pero yo no establezco los presupuestos: Reacciono a ellos.

En general, en este país no valoramos el paisaje o los espacios públicos. Un reflejo de esto es la utilización de materiales baratos. Intento darle algo de aliento a un lugar que generalmente está devaluado o subvaluado, y de imbuir el paisaje con algo de magia o significado, que trascienda el hecho de que su dueño sólo quiere gastar 23 dólares por pie cuadrado. Eso es menos de lo que se gasta en una alfombra.

El tratar de encontrar virtud en materiales bajos y que no sean caros, es inevitable si uno desea avanzar hacia el futuro con optimismo. El mundo no va a volver atras a riqueza centralizada, ni a la tradición artesanal. No vamos avolver a atras a tallar piedra. La desaparición de la artesanía es parte de la democratización, de destribucion de la riqueza. Vivimos en una época en la cual todos tendran que conformarse con pedazos más pequeños del pastel.

Muchas de las elecciones que hacemos en términos de materiales, reflejan un cierto nivel de deshonestidad cultural. Me encuentro con esto seguido. Frecuentemente los clientes se sienten incomodos con materiales de poca calidad, pero dispuestos o pueden aumentar el presupuesto para satisfacer sus propios estanderes. Esto nos lleva a lo que yo llamo el "problema de apariencias." Por ejemplo, un cliente puede decirte que quiere que algo se "vea" como granito, lo que significa que quiere que la gente perciba algo que no existe. El objetivo, que se espera que yo, como la diseñadora, voy a apoyar, es el de diseñar un ambiente que crea la impresión de que el proyecto es más caro de lo que es. En tanto que el concreto estampado se "vea" como piedra, se cumplió el objetivo.

Yo encuentro eso terriblemente deshonesto. Yo no estoy en el negocio de tratar de engañar a la gente. Si usted sólo puede pagar concreto prensado, entonces la pregunta es, ¿cómo se puede aplicar ese concreto prensado para apoyar una idea? Debiera ser un medio de expresión, no un instrumento para engañar a alguien, o para presentar una fachada para el engreimiento de alguien en cuanto a quien le gustaría ser, o qué quisiera que los otros creyeran que son. Creo que cualquier diseño o cualquier obra de arte de importancia, tiene integridad.

Con frecuencia, el arte es una exploración de aquello que es esencial, puro o primario – la comunicacion un estado de ánimo, sentimiento o una idea, es necesaria si el arte tenga impacto sobre la cultura. Lo más directa y honesta uno puede ser en una exprecion, la comunicación será más directa. El plástico no me molesta en lo absoluto, a menos que uno este tratando que alguien crea que es cuero. La deshonestidad y la presuntuosidad intelectual, indican que la gente está incomoda con ser quien es. Cuando un diseñador trata de engañar a otros creando una apariencia que nos separe cada vez mas de entender quiénes somos.

¿Cuál es su respuesta a los críticos que opinan que usted no es una arquitecta paisajista porque no le gustan las plantas?

Utilizo plantas cuando la situacion lo requiere. Nuevamente, mucha gente no entiende el enorme compromiso que significa hacer un paisaje, especialmente en una situacion urbana. Para poder crear un paisaje sobre una cochera o en una terraza, debes introducir más acero para sostener su peso; tal construccion es muy cara, y además hay que cuidarla. Tener un paisaje es como decidir tener un hijo o una mascota: si no se tiene el dinero suficiente para construir o cuidar el proyecto y adecuadamente, entonces no deberías tenerlo. Si no hay plantas en nuestros proyectos, esto significa generalmente, que no hay presupuesto o que no hay la posibilidad de darles mantenimiento.

Usted trabaja con una gama de colores brillantes, ¿podría hablarnos acerca del modo en que incorpora el color a sus diseños paisajistas?

Siempre me han gustado los colores brillantes, desde que era una niña, es lo mismo que cuando nos gustan los dulces. Una de mis abuelas sentía un placer infantil por los colores. Me traía baratijas brillantes de Florida y tenía patos de yeso y flores de plástico en su patio durante todo el año. Cuando los patios de todos los demás estaban grises y llenos de nieve, ella tenía manchas de flores de hermosos colores. Cuando era una niña, no juzgaba criticamente su jardín como algo artificial o falto de buen gusto sobre todo en un clima gris como el del noreste de Filadelfia. Yo disfrutaba esos colores tanto como ella.

Siempre me ha sido un placer ver colores. Nunca me he permitido que ese placer se acabe. Es importante conservar dentro de uno mismo algunas de las calidades infantiles. Todavía me emociono al ver colores brillantes, y en el exterior se ven aún más espléndidos.

Al crecer, aprendemos lo que para otros es de buen gusto y aceptable. Aprendemos a no entusiasmarnos con colores fuertes, relucientes, que son la gama visual que nos presentan cuando somos pequeños. Todo el tema del buen gusto me resulta repugnante. El "gusto" es un conjunto establecido de reglas sobre cómo debemos vernos, actuar y sentir. Nuestra cultura es fóbica con respecto a los colores tambien. La falta de color en nuestra cultura es un vestigio del norte europeo. Cuando la gente ve un color brillante, con frecuencia se sienten felices o aliviados. Es como una señal que les permite ser más libres en su manera de actuar. Es sorprendente lo poderoso que puede ser una señal de color y lo rápidamente que puede transmitir un estado de ánimo.

¿Quiénes son los arquitectos paisajistas cuyo trabajo admira usted?

Tal vez mi mayor inspiración proviene de la obra de Isamu Noguchi. Cuando empecé a estudiar paisajes, influyeron mucho en mí sus esculturas horizontales sobre formaciones de tierra y sus escenarios para Martha Graham. Noguchi trascendió los límites entre arte, diseño y paisaje. Sus paisajes crean lugares mágicos, surrealistas.

Usted ha escrito que el arte de la arquitectura paisajista consiste en definir la relación entre naturaleza y cultura. ¿Puede comentar algo sobre esto?

Yo quiero utilizar el paisaje para hablar del hecho de ser humanos, para comunicar ideas. Los paisajes que, en mi opinión, son los más maravillosos, son aquellos que identifican algo acerca de nuestra naturaleza humana y nos la reflejan. Contemplar un hermoso paisaje es como mirar un espejo o un retrato.

Muchas personas escuchan el término "paisaje" y piensan que es sinónimo de "naturaleza." Los paisajes naturales juegan un rol importante en nuestra cultura, pero lo que más me interesa es el paisaje que hacemos y ocupamos. En mi trabajo, la pregunta que siempre hago es: "¿Cómo refleja el paisaje quienes somos y quienes queremos ser?"

Siempre me ha gustado trabajar con materiales que tienen vida de acuerdo a nuestras necesidades. Me fascina utilizar espacios exteriores como "habitaciones" que podamos habitar. Me intrigan los paisajes en los que los árboles se utilizan para hacer corredores, donde los viñedos se convierten en refugios y lo setos verdes forman habitaciones. Me encantan mucho estos lugares transitorios que, no son ni naturaleza, ni arquitectura.

Yo crecí en Filadelfia. Solíamos ir a Longwood Gardens a visitar invernaderos increíbles que incluían jardines formales con pisos hechos de césped. Yo fantaseaba con vivir en una casa donde me levantara en las mañanas y que mis pies, lo primero que tocaran, fuera una alfombra de césped. No creo que transformar la naturaleza para satisfacer nuestras necesidades, sea automáticamente destructivo, si consideramos a los humanos como parte de la naturaleza. Yo creo que podemos y debemos formar ciudades, casas y habitaciones —lugares para comer y relajarse, lugares para vivir—con los elementos del paisaje.

Su amor por la naturaleza es por una naturaleza controlada. ¿Qué opina de Yosemite, por ejemplo?

Para mí, la belleza de las ideas es tan significativa como la belleza de la naturaleza. El poder y la belleza de las ideas me llenan de energía. Me encantan las ciudades: son las depositarias de la cultura. Me emociona más lo que puedo ver y oír en Nueva York, que lo que pueda ver y oír en Yosemite.

Claro que nunca diría que la naturaleza agreste no es importante; creo que es importante de una manera abstracta. Todos necesitamos saber que la naturaleza agreste existe —que si tuviéramos que vivir ahí, podríamos. Pero actualmente, pocos de nosotros sabemos lo que es la verdadera naturaleza salvaje— es una idea abstracta para la mayoría de los norteamericanos. Para llegar a esta naturaleza salvaje hay que hacer un gran esfuerzo; hay que subirse a un avión y después a un auto. La estancia ahí es breve y entonces hay que regresar. Creo que tal vez podríamos ser felices con una naturaleza salvaje virtual —en la pantalla de una computadora o en otra modalidad de realidad virtual. Estar en la naturaleza salvaje es una experiencia mucho más abstracta que vivir en una ciudad o en un barrio residencial periférico. La naturaleza salvaje es una fantasía romántica que llevamos dentro de nosotros, pero no es parte de nuestra realidad.

Desafortunadamente, mucha de la resistencia a la arquitectura paisajista, tiene que ver con la fantasía norteamericana sobre la naturaleza salvaje. A pesar de que nos imaginamos viviendo en la hermosa naturaleza salvaje, hemos permitido que se disemine una enorme fealdad en el paisaje. Estamos tan cegados por nuestra fantasía sobre la naturaleza salvaje, que cualquier cosa que no sea agreste, se desatiende o se olvida. Ya que un centro comercial no es agreste, su paisaje no merece ningún trato especial; está bien que esté rodeado por un estacionamiento sin árboles.

La idea de que el estacionamiento de un centro comercial pudiera convertirse en un paisaje viable e interesante, capaz de modificar el medio ambiente, es una idea que los norteamericanos no han descubierto. No queremos gastar dinero, ni legislar o invertir tiempo y esfuerzo, para lograr que un paisaje y un estacionamiento se diseñen juntos.

Usted ha escrito que tratamos al paisaje de la misma manera que los victorianos clasificaban a las mujeres: como vírgenes o como rameras.

Así es. La gente compartimenta el paisaje en su mente, se piensa en el paisaje como una mera reliquia de la naturaleza. El "paisaje" existe en los parques y en Yosemite. La idea de que los paisajes existan como estacionamientos, azoteas o franjas estrechas de terreno en líneas divisorias, no es fácil que la gente lo imagine. La "naturaleza" implica imágenes pintorescas; permitimos que nuestros paisajes, si no son pintorescos o naturales, se deterioren indiscriminadamente. Realmente no hemos inventado un nombre para los paisajes que hemos creado para vivir ahí.

¿Existen otras culturas o civilizaciones que sean mejores para dar forma al paisaje público?

Son mucho mejores las culturas de Francia, Alemania, Holanda, España, Japón e Italia. Nuestro fracaso es, tal vez, el más decepcionante porque somos muy ricos y capaces. Muchos países tienen tal necesidad de desarrollo que su descuido del paisaje, aunque deplorable, es comprensible. Es difícil convencer a la gente para que construya de una manera ecológica, responsable y bella, cuando necesitan desarrollo, empleos, comercio.

Por otra parte, nosotros debemos ser más previsores al evaluar nuestro paisaje. Tenemos los medios para crear un medio ambiente que corresponda a nuestro estilo de vida. Al hablar de medio ambiente incluyo nuestros paisajes urbanos, agrícolas y de zonas residenciales periféricas. Países como Francia y Holanda están mucho más adelantados en lo que se refiere a pensar en el paisaje como espacios exteriores que incluyen y responden al uso humano.

¿Qué es lo que los artistas y los diseñadores hacen de una manera diferente en esos países?

Holanda tiene actualmente algunos de los mejores arquitectos paisajista a nivel mundial. Los holandeses nos llevan ventaja porque han elaborado su paisaje desde el principio —el territorio que ocupan lo crearon del océano. Son más libres para pensar cómo manejar el paisaje, porque ellos lo han construido desde el principio.

En la mayoría de los países europeos, las áreas donde vive la gente —carreteras, ferrocarriles y calles de la ciudad— son mucho más hermosas que las nuestras. Estos países apoyan a sus artistas y diseñadores, lo que demuestra el valor que tiene la cultura en cuanto a la calidad del medio ambiente visual. Por ejemplo, los franceses se identifican con su paisaje construido y se ven a través de él. Sin embargo, nosotros no lo hacemos. Vemos el arte y el diseño como un accesorio —la cereza en el pastel. Los norteamericanos no perciben el centro comercial en una franja angosta de terreno en la periferia de todas nuestras ciudades, como símbolos de nuestra identidad nacional. No nos identificamos de esa manera con la tierra. Nos identificamos con las imágenes de fantasía de paisajes pintorescos en las carteleras publicitarias, en anuncios de revistas o en la televisión, pero nunca con los lugares donde vivimos.

Nuestras carreteras, puentes, vías públicas, parques e infraestructura, son vistos como un medio ambiente que es práctico, donde el arte no es necesario ni tiene cabida. Cada vez que me bajo de un avión, después de haber visitado otros países, me doy cuenta de lo estrecha que es nuestra visión de lo que es esencial en la vida. Como valor, la funcionalidad reina sobre la belleza. Somos una nación que tiene poco interés en esto, y esto es notorio.

¿Cómo se propone crear un clima donde se acepte valorar el paisaje construido? ¿Cómo podemos aprender a valorar estacionamientos, centros comerciales en franjas estrechas de terreno y líneas divisorias?

No soy predicadora, sin embargo, doy clases y espero que lo que construyo logre que el paisaje sea visible para aquellos que generalmente no lo ven. Tal vez pueda presentar esto como un área de oportunidades para aquellos que quieran explorar el paisaje, como diseñadores o como artistas. Con frecuencia siento que simplemente estoy reaccionando al mercado, pero casi siempre, proyecto tras proyecto, termino educando al cliente en cuanto a las posibilidades inherentes en el paisaje. Es un proceso lento.

Es muy difícil enseñarle a alguien el valor del arte y del diseño, si no ha tenido una capacitación previa o si no ha tenido contacto con ambos. Muchos de mis clientes son muy inteligentes y bien preparados en la mayoría de las áreas; pero frecuentemente no tienen las bases para entender las ideas visuales. Simplemente no tienen información sobre el tema del arte. En este país, ya no se enseña historia ni arte en las escuelas. Si en casa no se tiene contacto con las ideas estéticas, son pocas las oportunidades de educarse uno mismo a través de la cultura. Otras culturas abarcan un enfoque más integral en cuanto a la estética. En los Estados Unidos, la falta de comprensión y apoyo general con respecto a lo que hacemos, representa un dilema para muchos arquitectos paisajistas, artistas y arquitectos. ¿Tomamos un avión y nos vamos a Japón porque los japoneses valoran el papel de la estética en el medio ambiente? ¿O debemos intentar buscar interés y apoyo aquí? Si decidimos concentrar nuestro trabajo en Estados Unidos, ¿qué hacemos en una era de recursos cada vez más limitados?

En una de sus conferencias, usted le dijo al público que está buscando empresas e instituciones que apoyen esta idea de mejorar el medio ambiente construido. ¿Ya encontró alguna?

Ya he realizado algunas obras para la Administración de Servicios Generales (GSA por sus siglas en inglés); pero aún en obras públicas, se necesita que una persona quiera arriesgarse y apoyarte. Desafortunadamente, la mayoría de la gente que trabaja en el servicio público, no están dispuestos a correr el riesgo. La gente vota por ellos, se les supervisa, no son autónomos, así que encontrar a alguien que te apoye a través de todo el proceso, es una tarea muy difícil. Se necesita alguien que esté comprometido con la idea de que uno, como artista o diseñador, tiene una contribución importante que hacer al medio ambiente.

Estamos a punto de terminar una serie de proyectos del gobierno —la Plaza Jacob Javits en Manhattan, la plaza del HUD en Washington, D.C., y una plaza para la nueva Corte que se está construyendo en Minneapolis, estos proyectos son una enorme oportunidad. Los proyectos del gobierno son conocidos por ser anodinos y nada controversiales, basados en la idea de que los proyectos públicos deben estar de acuerdo con el criterio de todos los usuarios. Esto siempre da como resultado un diseño que ha sido reducido al mínimo común denominador, para evitar problemas políticos. Para mí, estos proyectos son un experimento para saber si es posible hacer obras públicas interesantes y audaces. Ninguno de estos proyectos es caro, todo tiene que verificarse. En la GSA tenemos un patrocinador progresista, él está ahí para asegurarse de que no se pierda lo estético, de que la esencia artística esté presente como un componente importante.

¿Existe un común denominador en los proyectos de la GSA?

Estas plazas —Javits, HUD, Minneapolis— son plazas típicas, construidas en la década de los años sesenta, alrededor de edificios. De acuerdo con los principios modernistas de esa época, los edificios se levantaban en el espacio como heroicos objetos escultóricos, asentados sobre el nivel del terreno vacío y utópico. Típicamente, los arquitectos eliminaban todo lo que estuviera cerca del edificio para evitar la competencia con su forma escultórica. Las plazas vacías encima de los estacionamientos, producían espacios muertos en la parte de abajo de los edificios. A través de los años, la gente ha tratado de ocupar estos espacios infructuosamente.

Muchas de nuestras zonas céntricas más importantes, se construyeron en la era expansionista de la década de los años sesenta, cuando se construyeron estas plazas vacías. El posmodernismo criticó estos espacios. Decidimos que, después de todo, tal vez el muro de la calle era útil, que esas grandes plazas solitarias, creaban vacíos y que deberíamos crear más espacios humanitarios en la parte de abajo de los edificios. Se cuestionó la primacía de los edificios como escultura. Ha habido una nueva evaluación y un intento de volver a adecuar y habitar estos espacios.

Estos tres proyectos de la GSA transmiten todos ellos un humor irónico y desenfadado. ¿Qué papel juega el humor en sus diseños?

Toda mi familia tiene un gran sentido del humor. Quizá proviene de la tradición judía —el humor, es una poderosa herramienta que ayuda a las personas a dar la cara a problemas que es doloroso enfrentar. El viejo refrán de que "la comedia es un asunto muy serio," es absolutamente cierto. La mayoría de las grandes comedias surgen de la ira; he observado que los comediantes, con frecuencia, son las personas más enojadas. Yo también soy una persona bastante iracunda, parece que la ira me activa. El humor es un método socialmente aceptable de ventilar la ira y la frustración. El humor abre a la gente —son más receptivos, les encanta que los hagan reír por algo— es un descanso.

Háblenos sobre su diseño de la Plaza Jacob Javits, donde antes se ubicaba el "Tilted Arc" de Richard Serra.

Nuestra versión de la Plaza Javits es una reacción a la escultura del "Tilted Arc". Quería que fuera la antítesis del "Tilted Arc" —menos importante en sí mismo y menos auto alusivo. Es más modesta en sus ambiciones: es sólo una plaza agradable para sentarse y comer. El "Tilted Arc" era una crítica a la arquitectura modernista y una expresión de alejamiento; era una fuerte confrontación. En nuestra Plaza Javits, no tiene uno que entrar en controversia, sencillamente se puede sentar a comer ahí.

El arte público del mundo aprendió mucho a través de las pruebas del "Tilted Arc." El uso de la plaza fue trastocado por la visión del artista, y la pregunta de si esa subversión es adecuada para el arte público, se convirtió en una valiosa discusión. Durante esa secuencia de eventos, yo cambié de opinión sobre qué debe ser el arte público. Tiene que funcionar en varios niveles, no es una galería de arte. La gente no tiene que elegir si ocuparse de él o no. El mejor arte público es aquel que puede hablar en muchos niveles, y si alguien decide no ocuparse de él, no tiene que hacerlo.

¿Qué consejo daría a los funcionarios públicos que están tratando de mejorar los espacios urbanos?

A la mayoría de los lugares públicos se les ignora y se abusa de ellos, sus diseños son insulsos y burdos. No se ha logrado un sentido de ubicación, principalmente porque no se han corrido riesgos. Se necesita valor para apoyar una idea, pero los proyectos públicos, generalmente están en el ámbito de los funcionarios públicos, que son especialmente vulnerables al escrutinio. Si queremos plazas, parques, calles, estacionamientos y azoteas que la gente pueda sentir como propias, es indispensable que los funcionarios públicos exijan más a los diseñadores de estos espacios. Les exigimos a los arquitectos, pero la arquitectura paisajista no se ha visualizado como una forma de arte. Es importante que los funcionarios públicos establezcan parámetros más altos y exijan que estos espacios, tengan personalidad y espíritu; porque para que el paisaje sea funcional, la gente debe disfrutarlo, emocional y espiritualmente.

¿Podría hablarnos sobre los costos psicológicos para los norteamericanos, ocasionados por nuestros desprestijiados paisajes? Usted ha dicho que sanear nuestros paisajes podría ayudar a sanear nuestras patologías sociales.

Creo que el medio ambiente en el que vivimos, definitivamente forma parte toral de cómo nos definimos y de qué esperamos, de cuáles son nuestras esperanzas. La gente reacciona automáticamente a algo hermoso, no es algo que se aprenda viendo diapositivas. La gente responde a la calidad del espacio, a la proporción del espacio, al color, la luz, el ritmo, la textura. No se necesita mucho para imaginar el efecto psicológico en una persona que se muda de una vecindad urbana a una hermosa habitación llena de luz y aire, o quien va de una calle de un estacionamiento de un estrecho centro comercial a los Campos Elíseos.

Tendemos a pensar que la gente no ve o no siente esas diferencias, pero sí lo hacen. La gente vive mejor en lugares que se ven y se sienten mejor. No somos animales viviendo en la selva, somos seres humanos.

El arte es una medida para la salud. Si el arte florece en una cultura, esto significa que las necesidades básicas para vivir, están satisfechas: tener un techo, no estar en guerra, tener un gobierno estable, tener comida, que exista un cierto grado de predictibilidad: una vez que todo eso está resuelto, ¿qué hacen? Sueñan, escriben, pintan, hacen jardines. La jardinería es un verdadero lujo, es por eso que muy pocas culturas realmente han desarrollado una jardinería autóctona, vernácula. Se necesita una cultura estable y rica para producir este medio ambiente. Mi frustración es que nosotros, como norteamericanos, podríamos crear un mejor medio ambiente para nosotros, pero decidimos no hacerlo.

¿Puede hablarnos sobre su utilización de la geometría en el paisaje?

Las líneas y los ángulos correctos son hechos por el hombre. Cuando imponemos un orden geométrico en el paisaje, ocupamos el paisaje con el pensamiento humano. La geometría define claramente algo artificial, más que un medio ambiente natural. Si usted quisiera que lean o vean algo en el caos inherente de la naturaleza, la manera más rápida de lograrlo sería aplicar el orden geométrico. La geometría es también una extensión de la ciudad, una manera de integrar las obras construidas a un mapa ya existente.

Estoy interesada en organizar la experiencia personal a través del espacio. Esto no es fácil hacerlo en el exterior, debido a la escala, que es mucho mayor que la escala arquitectónica y por la naturaleza caótica del espacio exterior. Internamente guardamos formas geométricas, como mapas en la cabeza —podemos recordar cómo se ve un círculo o un cuadrado. Así que si uno pone esas formas en el suelo, es una manera de orientar a la gente en el espacio. En cambio, si la gente se encuentra con una silueta amébica o naturalista con la que no han tenido una experiencia previa, es mucho más perturbador. Una persona nunca está segura de dónde está; en el espacio exterior necesita mapas mentales conocidos.

Por ejemplo, el Citadel es un paisaje altamente ordenado, un paisaje consecutivo en el que se repiten formas conocidas. Esa repetición produce una referencia al espacio arquitectónico y define una habitación. La habitación en cuyo interior ocurre algo, es un tema común en mi trabajo, ya que las habitaciones se hacen con el propósito de que los humanos las habiten. Esto, por sí mismo, es un fuerte contraste con la naturaleza.

¿Cuál es su definición de jardín?

Un jardín, como lo contrario a paisaje, es un lugar que da un sentido de separación del mundo exterior. La separación se debe crear al formar un umbral —ya sea real o implícito. Este umbral crea la posibilidad de dejar un mundo y entrar a otro. Esa es la función fundamental de un jardín: darle a una persona el espacio psicológico para soñar, pensar, descansar o desconectarse del mundo. Funciona como una interrupción de la rutina diaria, como entrar a una iglesia o a un templo. Tiene el propósito de describir otro tipo de espacio psicológico, ayudarte a tocar tu yo verdadero.

¿Cuál es el pronóstico para la arquitectura del paisaje en Estados Unidos?

Tenemos que redefinir lo que consideramos que es el paisaje. Yo considero paisaje cualquier cosa que esté fuera de un edificio —el camino, la carretera, el estacionamiento, y todo lo demás. Si sólo la vemos como auxiliar de la arquitectura —parques, jardines y plazas— entonces la arquitectura paisajista se va a convertir en una profesión mucho más marginalizada. Tenemos que concentrarnos en ser más útiles. Debemos comprometernos con proyectos menos glamorosos, menos orientados hacia el prestigio y empezar a ocuparnos de nuestro paisaje, física y visualmente degradado. Ese es nuestro futuro. Diseñar jardines para gente rica puede ser muy bien pagado, pero no será suficiente para conservar una profesión vital.

Vivir en un mundo ambientalmente balanceado se está volviendo cada vez más importante. Sin embargo, hay mucha gente que siente que el diseño no es importante para hacer el paisaje ambientalmente sano. Creo que esos son extremos falsos que establece la profesión. Mi esperanza es que nuestra sensibilidad hacia nuestro medio ambiente, algún día incluirá el darnos cuenta de la calidad visual de todos nuestros medios ambientes construidos. Ese va a ser nuestro papel: crear un medio ambiente sano y fuerte que también sea un lugar hermoso y significativo para los seres humanos.

Die Verwandlung des Alltäglichen

Elisabeth K. Meyer

Elisabeth K. Meyer ist Landschaftsarchitektin und Professorin an der Universität von Virginia, wo sie die Graduiertenabteilung für Landschaftsarchitektur leitet. Sie unterrichtet Design Werkstätten und bietet einen Kurs über Theorie und Praxis der modernen Landschaftsarchitektur an. Bevor sie nach Virginia kam, gehörte Meyer der Fakultät der Harvard Universität an und arbeitete mit folgenden Firmen der Landschaftsarchitektur: Michael Vergasonand Associates, Hanna/Olin, und EDAW Alexandria.

Der Bagel-Garten, Back Bay, Boston, Massachusetts

"Eine petite parterre Verzierung ist in bestehenden Hecken angelegt. Zwei konzentrische Vierecke aus 16 Zoll hohem Buchsbaum. Zwischen dem inneren und dem äußeren Viereck befindet sich ein 30 Zoll breiter Streifen aus lila Kies, auf dem ein Gitternetz wetterfester Bagels (jüdisch-amerikanische rundeTeigware aus weichem Weißbrot mit einem Loch in der Mitte) sitzt. Im Zentrum des inneren Vierecks sind 30 lila Ageratum in Sechserreihen angeflanzt, so daß sie das lila Farbmuster umgekehrt wiedergeben."

-Martha Schwartz, Projektbeschreibung

Der New York City Blumenzwiebelgarten

"Dieses Pflanzenbeet wird zunächst zwecks des guten Abflußes mit 2 Zoll Kies gefüllt, dann mit 12 Zoll leichter Mischerde und schließlich mit 4 Zoll Sand abgedeckt. Es wird 4712 sechs Zoll hohe Blumentöpfe enthalten, in welchen jeweils eine von vier verschiedenen Knollenarten steckt. Diese Töpfe werden gemäß einem Plan für jede Art in dem Pflanzenbecken angeordnet. Ihre aufeinanderfolgenden Blütezeiten buchstabieren die Worte "Habgier", "Übel", "Ignoranz" und "Seligkeit", ein Kommentar zum zeitgenössischen städtischen Leben.Um die Blumenzwiebel richtig zu plazieren, hat jeder Blumentopf eine besondere Nummer, die ihn an eine nummerierte Position verweist. Die für dieses Schema ausgesuchten Knollen sind Osterglocken, griechische Annemonen, peruanische Lilien und Amaryllis. Sie blühen im Frühjahr, im Sommer, im frühen und im späten Herbst. Die Knollen wurden wegen ihrer niedrigen Pflegebedürftigkeit und ihrer Toleranz gegenüber Frost und kalten Temperaturen ausgesucht. Der Garten kann mit einem Gartenschlauch bewässert werden."

-Marta Schwartz, in Transforming the American Garden (1986)

Von Martha Schwartz kreierte Landschaften sind Zusammenstellungen alltäglicher Gegenstände und Materialien, wie man sie in Eisenhandlungen oder Gartenbedarfskatalogen finden kann: Blumentöpfe, farbige Kieselsteine, Plastikblumen, Kunstrasen, Gartenornamente (reflektierende Globen und vergoldete Frösche), grellgelbe "Parken verboten" Farbe, Kalkstaub, Faden und Klebeband. Obwohl einige dieser Materialien und Mittel nicht gerade Bestandteile einer Landschaftsarchitektur sind, die es anstrebt permanent und ernsthaft zu sein, rechnet Schwartz ihre Arbeit dennoch zu diesem Fachgebiet.In ihren Projektbeschreibungen entdeckt man durchweg die räumlichen und formalen Werkzeuge des Gartendesignerseine petite parterre Verzierung, Alleen, Heckenreihen, Haine, Erdhügel und Terrassen.Diese Einbeziehung von Alltäglichem und Profanem, der Fertigware und des Provisorischen in das Gebiet der Landschaftsarchitektur verursacht die Ereiferung der Berufsmitglieder mit der Veröffenlichung jedes neuen Projektes. Die Arbeiten von Schwartz, besonders die der 80er Jahre, wurden als Übertretungen dessen interpretiert, was für Landschaftsarchitektur angemessen war, und schlimmer noch, als ironische Kommentare zum Befinden des Berufes verschrien. Die Kritiker hatten in beiden Fällen Recht. Ihre Arbeit war eine Form von gebauter Kritik, die gleichzeitig existierende Normen angriff, als auch neue Konzepte der Landschaftsgestaltung durchsetzte.

Schwartz war und bleibt weiterhin verblüfft über das Trara, das ihre Arbeit verursacht. Immerhin vergnügten sich Künstler in den späten 70er und fruehen 80er Jahren mit weitaus provozierenderen Aktivitäten, als dem Lackieren von 8 Dutzend Bagels und deren Arrangement auf einem Feld von Aquariumkies im eigenen Vorgarten. "Zu jener Zeit kreuzigte sich der Künstler Chris Burden auf VW Dächern, und Vito Acconci onanierte hinter Treppen; folglich schien mir dies keine große Sache," erklärte Schwartz während eines Vortrags im Jahre 1995.[5] Sie interpretierte die Reaktion auf ihre frühen Arbeiten als das Symptom eines "schlafwandelnden" Berufsfeldes, einer Gruppe von Praktizierenden, die davor zurückschreckt, Aufmerksamkeit auf sich oder ihr Gebiet zu lenken.Eine Designpraxis, die Räume im ökologischen Kontext schafft, wo sie am sichtbarsten sind, sich dann aber meistens als unsichtbarer Hintergrund verlieren. Die Resonanz der Kollegen auf Schwartzens Arbeiten ist teilweise durch diese Gesinnung zu erklären. Sie ist aber ebenso symptomatisch für ein kreatives Gebiet, das die Richtlinien einer Disziplin überschreitet, oder genauer gesagt, welches das begriffliche Territorium zweier Disziplinen beansprucht, in diesem Falle das der zeitgenössischen Kunst und der Landschaftsarchitektur. Schwartzens Überschreitungsakt bedroht die Integrität und die Autonomie einer Berufsbezeichnung, irritiert diejenigen, die klare Grenzdefinitionen brauchen und verletzt die innere Logik eine Gebietes.

Warum, fragt man sich, sollte ein Künstler oder Designer diesen Schritt gehen wollen? Die Antwort spricht aus Schwartzens Arbeiten. Diese Art von Überschreitungstaktiken verfremdet das Vertraute: in den Worten des Philosophen und Kunstkritikers Arthur Danto, sie "wandeln den Alltäglich um." Sie katapultieren uns aus einem Stadium der Abwesenheit und zwingen uns wahrzunehmen, lebendig zu sein und unsere Umgebung zur Notiz zu nehmen. Für die Mitglieder eines Berufes, dessen Abgrenzung durch derartige Umwandlungstendenzen unter Beschuß steht, ist dies Aufrüttelung kombiniert mit der intellektuellen Offenbarung, daß die bis dahin statischen Konventionen des Berufes, nun nicht nur in Frage gestellt, sondern beleuchtet und somit zum ersten Mal erkenntlich gemacht werden. Danto erklärt dieses Phänomen in einer Diskussion über Andy Warhols Gebrauch von alltäglichen Gegenständen:

> Diese Umwandlung eines gewöhnlichen Objektes verändert in der Kunstwelt gar nichts. Sie bringt nur die Strukturen der Kunst zur Geltung, welche sicherlich eine gewisse geschichtliche Entwicklung brauchten, bevor diese Metapher möglich war. In dem Moment wo sie möglich war, war soetwas wie die Brillo Box unvermeidbar und sinnlos. Sie war ein unweigerliches Geschehen, das einfach passieren mußte, ob nun mit diesem oder jenem Objekt.[6]

Aus dieser Perspektive gesehen, wirken die Projekte einer Martha Schwartz wie eine Art Zauberball oder reflektierender Himmelskörper auf ihr Berufsfeld. Sie markieren einen bestimmten Raum, verwickeln aber gleichzeitig ein erweitertes Gebiet und andere Designer damit. Jedesmal wenn Schwartz das Alltägliche mit gewöhnlichen Mitteln verwandelt, sehen wir unsere Arbeit, unsere Werte und unsere Einstellung in einem neuen Licht.

Was bedeutet es, die Grenzen von Landschaftsarchitektur heraus zu fordern?

Warum wirkt Schwartzens Arbeit so provozierend? Ein Grund dafür ist das Maß in welchem sie nicht nur das Fach der Landschaftsarchitektur, sondern auch die Definition von Landschaft an sich, herausfordert. Jetzt sind wir uns bewußt, daß Landschaft ein dehnbarer Begriff ist. In vielen seiner Schriften, besonders im Aufsatz "The Word Itself"[7], verfolgt J.B. Jackson die Entwicklung der Bedeutung von Landschaft. Er bietet eine neue Definition an, die einen unbequemen Rahmen für Schwartzens Arbeiten aufwirft:

> Eine Komposition künstlicher oder veränderter Landschaft, die als Infrastruktur oder Hintergrund für unser kollektives Dasein dient; und falls Hintergrund unpassend bescheiden erscheint, sollten wir uns daran erinnern, daß der moderne Gebrauch des Wortes das beschreibt, was nicht nur unsere Identität und Gegenwart, sondern auch unsere Geschichte ausmacht.[8]

In ihrer visuellen Klarheit und Eindrücklichkeit sind die meisten Schwartz'sche Landschaften, wie beispielsweise das Rio Einkaufszentrum oder der HUD Hauptquartierplatz, alles andere als bloßer Hintergrund. Sie sind sozusagen vielleicht Buhnenbild für Aktion, aber auf keinen Fall stiller Hintergrund. Weiterhin behandelt Jackson die Tendenz der Amerikaner Landschaft als Synonym für natürliche Szenerie, für pastorale oder malerische Darstellung zu sehen. Wir verstehen Landschaft im Allgemeinen als eine Gegebenheit: vielen von uns fällt gar nicht auf, dass die ländlichen Szenerien, die wir so schätzen, menschlicher Manipulation entspringen:sie sind geformt, modelliert, und gepflegt. Im Gegensatz zu den Briten, sehen wir Landschaft als naturgegeben, nicht als konstruiert.

Schwartzens Arbeiten aus synthetischen Fertigteilen, angeordnet in starken Figuren oder Geometrien der Wiederholung oder Serienmäßigkeit und mit verstecktem Witz versehen,

sind bewußte, kulturelle Konstruktionen. Sie fordern die Denkkategorien heraus, die den Beruf und die populäre Definition von Landschaftsarchitektur strukturieren: natürlich gegenüber kulturell, dauerhaft gegenüber vergänglich, echt gegenüber synthetisch, ernst gegenüber ironisch und Hintergrund gegenüber Vordergrund. Diese Herausforderung an die Definition von Landschaft erhöht das Risiko für die Landschaftsarchitektur. Unzufrieden damit einen bloßen Hintergrund für Kunst und Leben zu schaffen, und stattdessen die Landschaft selbst Kunst und Leben reflektieren lassen zu wollen, schafft Schwartz Werke, die in der Landschaftsidee zweier britischer Geographen, Denis Cosgrove und Stephen Daniels, Resonanz finden. Sie schreiben:

> Landschaft ist eine kulturelle Idee, ein bildhafter Weg Umfeld zu repräsentieren, strukturieren und symbolisieren. Das soll nicht heißen, daß Landschaften unwirklich sind. Sie können in vielfältiger Weise und auf verschiedensten Oberflächen wiedergegeben werden - mit Farbe auf Leinwand, in Schrift auf Papier, mit Erde, Stein Wasser und Vegetation auf Grund und Boden.[9]

Schwartzens Bauprojekte fordern mehr von der Landschaft als nur Funktion.Die Räumlichkeit und Form einer Landschaft sollte immer auch wiederspiegeln, darstellen und symbolisieren, wie man die Welt sieht.

Herausforderungen an die Praxis der Landschaftsarchitektur des späten 20. Jahrhunderts.

Danto deutet an, daß Warhols Serie von Brillo Boxes die genormten Strukturen der Kunstdefinition und -kritik der 60er Jahre aufbrach. Schwartzens Poplandschaften haben denselben Effekt. Sie beleuchten die Strukturen und Bestimmungen mit Hilfe derer Landschaftsarchitekten die Art ihrer Projekte, die sie ansprechenden Plätze und ihre Designprinzipien definieren. Worin besteht nun die Herausforderung an ihre Haltung? Die erste ist etwas Grundsätzliches: die Praxis des Landschaftsarchitekten ist eng mit Kultur verbunden, da sie natürlich, künstlich als auch reell ist. Die Menschen nehmen die Welt durch eine kulturelle Brille wahr: wir schätzen Landschaft, Natur und Wildnis wegen ihrer Rollen in unserer Kultur. Anders ausgedrückt arbeiten wir im allgemeinen nicht mit einer jungfräulicher, unberührter Natur. Die zweite Herausforderung richtet sich an die Blindheit vieler Landschaftsarchitekten gegenüber dem Potential der vorgeformten Räumlichkeit heimischer Vorstadt- und Industrielandschaften, dem Designer Material und Inspiration zu liefern. Statt sich von diesen Asphaltlandschaften, Bauspekulationen, billigen Bauunternehmen und fraglichem Geschmack abzuwenden, sollte man ihren Einfluß auf den Geschmack der Masse erkennen. Projekte wie das Columbus Convention Center und das Center for Innovative Technologie geben genau das an Räumlichkeit und Material wieder, was man im Vorstadtcharakter, im Einkaufsstreifen und auf Parkplätzen findet.

Die dritte Herausforderung ist mit der zweiten verknüpft. Die Tendenz, das Gebiet des Landschaftsarchitekten auf Orte zu beschränken, die seiner Bemühung würdig scheinen, ist auffällig: Stadtparks, Firmenhauptquartiere und -plätze, edle Gärten, Universitätsgelände und so weiter. Man verbietet sich jegliche Zeitverschwendung auf einem Ort mit niedrigerem Prestige: der Parkplatz, der Mittelstreifen, der Autobahnauf und -abfahrt, dem übriggebliebenen Raum zwischen Gebäuden, den Innenhöfen. Diese Orte werden von ihren Besitzern als auch von Landschaftsarchitekten vernachläßigt. Folglich ist ihr Charakter ein Nebenprodukt anderweitig orientierter Entscheidungen oder der rein zweckgerichteten Ausführungen des Ingenieurs. Schwartz sieht diese Räume nicht nur als wesentlich, sondern als lebenswichtig für ihren Beruf an, besonders in Anbetracht der Tatsache, daß die angesehenen Projekte nicht groß an der Zahl, diese hingegen überzählig sind. Ihre Kommissionsausführungen der Citadel, des Whitehead Institutes und des Miami International Airport legen alle großen Wert auf Räume, die anderweitig als unsichtbar oder unwesentlich erklärt wurden und schaffen echte Umgebungen, wo sonst befremdende Territorien geblieben wären.

Schließlich muß man sagen, daß Schwartzens Materialpalette weder Natur noch verfeinerten Geschmack vorgaukelt. Statt einer langen Liste von Bäumen, Büschen, perenierenden Blumen, Granitbelägen und handgemachten Geländern, findet man gefärbten Zement, Asphalt, Farbe, Betonblöcke, Fiberglass, Kunstgras, Plexiglass, Verkehrsschilder, Eisenbahnschienen und -schwellen, Reifen und andere Fertigteile. Dieses Fehlen von Verfeinerung, dieses Begrüßen der gewöhnlichen (sozusagen abrufbaren und groben) Materialien beleidigt diejenigen, die diese Dinge mit kitschigen Vorstadtgärten und Industriegelänen assoziieren. Schwartz kontert mit dem Argument, daß dies die Materialien der Bauindustrie seien. Warum also nicht versuchen etwas Ehrliches und Schönes aus ihnen zu machen? Warum nicht versuchen, das Alltägliche zu verwandeln? Der Pragmatismus und die Popularität dieses Anliegens wird oft durch die Debatte über Stil und Schönheit verwässert. Wenn Danto Recht hat mit seiner Haltung, daß Schönheit "kein beschreibbarer Wert ist"[10], sondern in unserer Beziehung zur Welt besteht und vielleicht eine "Funktion dessen ist, was man über ein Objekt denkt"[11], dann sollten wir uns damit auseinandersetzen, warum wir diese Materalien und Gegenstände nicht höher schätzen. Diese Neigungen und Vorurteile limitieren im Grunde unsere Fähigkeit, neue Landschaftswelten zu kreieren oder uns neue Erscheinungsformen der Schönheit überhaupt vorzustellen.

Zusätzlich zu ihren Herausforderungen an das Fachgebiet der Landschaftsarchitektur, konfrontiert Schwartzens Praxis die Welt der Architekten in ihrer Tendenz, die Landschaftsfrage als Thema und als Raum an die Wand zu drücken. Diese rhetorische Herausforderung wird gegenwärtig am Neuentwurf von drei Platzen erprobt, die Exemplare spätmoderner Architektur sind, das Federal Courthouse in Minneapolis, das HUD (U.S. Department of Housing and Urban Development) in Washington,D.C. von Marcel Breuer in den 60er Jahren entworfen, und das Jacob Javits Federal Building in New York City. Diese Vorschläge sind Baukritiken an der Unterdrückung der Landschaft durch die moderne Architektur und ihre Verdammung zum bloßen Raum, zur tabula rasa, zum Podium für das skulpturelle Objekt Gebäude. Als Ersatz für diese verarmte Rolle bietet Schwartz der Architektur eine neue Reihe Konventionen für Landschaft an. Diese beinhalten die Erkenntnis, daß wir in Räumen leben, sowohl Innenräumen als auch Außenräumen, und daß Design nicht mit der Gebäudewand aufhören darf; daß ein Gebäude nur ein Objekt im Stilleben vieler Objekte ist; daß Landschaft wie Architektur nicht nur Form sondern auch Inhalt hat; und daß eine Fläche voll und nicht offen ist, bevor der Architekt ihn betritt. Schwartz ist ebenso aggressiv in der Überarbeitung dieser schwierigen, städtischen Orte, wie es die ihr vorangegangenen Architekten gewesen waren. In Washington D.C. verkörpert das von Breuer in den 60er Jahren entworfene HUD Hauptquartier die städtische Sensibilität jener Zeit. Dieses X-förmige Betongebäude erhebt sich auf Säulen inmitten eines sechs Acker grossen, ausdruckslosen Grundstückes. Schwartzens Projektvorschlag enthält nicht nur die Wiederbelebung des öffentlichen Platzes durch einen dreidimensionalen Teppich kreisrunder Pflanzbecken und Wandsitze mit farbigen Plastikscheiben als Schattenspender, sondern auch die Demolierung eines Teiles des Erdgeschoßes, um Verbindungen zwischen den vier voneinander abgetrennten Quadranten des Grundstücks zu schaffen. In New York City, wo zeitgenössische, städtische Landschaftsarchitektur darauf reduziert werden kann, aus der Liste der Parkabteilung die passenden Artikel zu bestellen, wie z.B. Weltausstellungsbänke, Laternenpfähle vom Central Park, schmiedeeiserne, ringförmige Beetbegrenzungen, Granitsitze und Pflastersteine beruft Schwartz sich auf eine andere Strategie, um die öffentliche Umgebung zu vergegenständlichen. Schwartzens Entwurf für den Jacob Javits-Platz spielt mit den Regeln und beinhaltet in ihren Worten "traditionelle New York Parkelemente mit humorvoller Komponenente"[12]. Diese Elemente sind nicht nur durch dimensionale Mutation (Laternenpfähle verjüngen sich von 12-30 Fuss Höhe), sondern auch durch ihre Zusammenstellung und Aneinanderreihung verwandelt. Normale Holzlattenbänke sind beispielsweise in langen, spiegelverkehrten Kurven angeordnet, die ein Muster schaffen, das der Roll- und Knotenverzierung eines französischen Blumenbeetes nicht unähnlich ist. Durch ihre Kreuzung von Parkmöbeln mit Gartenplanung bringt Schwartz Gilmore Clarke in die Welt des André Le Notre. Das Ergebnis ist ein Entwurf, der von seiner eigenen Zeit spricht, während er aus der Vergangenheit zitiert, ohne den Rückgriff auf generischen Zusammenhang, den wir in so vielen zeitgenössischen, öffentlichen Plätzen in New York City finden. Ein letztes Beispiel für diese aggressive Haltung gegenüber dem schon existierenden architektonischen Umfeld ist ihre Neigung, die vertikalen als auch die horizontalen Oberflächen zu bearbeiten. Der zeitweilig angelegte Turf Parterre Garten in Battery Park City als auch der Whitehead Institute Splice Garden in Cambridge, Massachusetts lassen ihre Muster und Gestik vom Boden in die Wände laufen, von der Horizontalen zur Vertikalen und übertreten damit die Grenzen, die für Landschaftsarchitekturkonstruktion und -form als angemessen betrachtet werden.

Das Werk der Martha Schwartz in ihrer Darstellung als postmoderne Praxis

Die Tendenz, die Traditionen eines Fachgebietes umzustülpen ist charakteristisch für viele kulturelle Tätigkeiten des späten 20. Jahrhunderts. Aus dieser Persplektive gesehen ist Schwartz eine typische Praktikerin der Postmoderne. Sie hat am Rande zweier Gebiete Raum zur Erneuerung entdeckt, und zwar im Spielraum zwischen der öffentlichen Kunst und der Landschaftsarchitektur. Indem sie ironischerweise Bilder und Materialien der Massenkultur mit ihrer Arbeit vermengt, hat Schwartz widerlegt, was Andreas Huyssen als die "grosse Scheide" zwischen hoher Kunst und Massenkultur bezeichnet, und hat damit ihre Position als Post-Modernist zementiert.[13] Dennoch sieht sie sich und ihre Arbeit in einem modernen Rahmen. Eine formale Analyse ihrer Arbeit bestätigt dies. Geometrische Formen wie Vierecke, Kreise und eiförmige Ovale schweben über Feldern, die durch die wiederkehrenden Muster eine gewisse Spannung bekommen. Gitter und deren dreidimensionale Erscheinungsform, Käfige, werden durch ihre Gegenüberstellung mit übergroßen Objekten betont. Der Ordnungsrahmen für abstrakte und minimalistische Kunst werden auf das Gebiet der Landschaftsarchitektur angepaßt und angewandt. Diese Anwendung moderner, formaler Mittel in einem neuen Zusammenhang, auf eine neue Konzeption, bezieht das aufeinander, was sich früher gegenseitig ausschloß, und was laut Huyssen das Zeichen moderner Praxis ist. Schwartzens Arbeit verkörpert die Weiterführung des Modernen und gleichzeitig ihre Kritik, die Einbeziehung der formalen Prinzipien moderner Kunst, als auch die respektlose Anwendung dieser Strategien in einer neuen Arena. Diese theoretische Perspektive ermöglicht es uns, Schwartz als eine zu sehen, die aus dem Beruf der Landschaftsarchitektur herausbricht. Sie stellt sie und die Arbeiten der Landschaftsarchitektur als aktive Beteiligte eines erweiterten kreativen und kulturellen Gebietes dar. Sie definiert Landschaftsarchitektur sowohl als eine kulturelle Praxis als auch als einen Beruf. Die Eingliederung von Schwartz als postmoderne, kulturell Praktizierende, die versucht das Moderne durch Verunreinigung und Neugravierung wieder zu beleben, bietet eine Alternative zur konservativen Haltung der postmodernen Praxis, die Modernität ablehnt und mit einer Art Geschichtlichkeit und Kontextualität zu ersetzten versucht. Wie verwandte Geister in der Kunst und Architektur z.B. Warhol und Robert Venturi oder Rem Koolhaas hat Schwartz auf der Suche nach Quellen für Inhalt und Verunreinigung ihren Blick auf den kommerziellen Markt, die Massenkultur, den Einkaufsstreifen und die Vorstadt gerichtet. Sie hat diese Eindrücke in ein neues Gebiet fließen lassen: die Kunst und Praxis von Garten und Landschaft. Darin liegt ihre Einzigartigkeit.

Martha Schwartz als Insider und Outsider

Trotz ihrer Verbindung zur zeitgenössischen Kunstpraxis, zu Gruppen innerhalb der Architektur und zu breit gefächerter postmoderner kultureller Praxis, hat Martha Schwartz wenig Gleichgesinnte in der zeitgenössischen Landschaftsarchitektur. Ungeachtet ihres Eintauchens in andere Fachgebiete wird Schwartzens Arbeit mit den Traditionen der Landschaftsarchitektur und dem Handwerk des Gartenbaus identifiziert. Da Blumenbeete, Rankengewächse und Büsche Bestandteile ihrer gebauten Visionen sind, ist ihre Arbeit aggressiv. Da ihre Landschaftsformen mit der Fachsprache und dem Ornament hoher Gartenkultur assoziiert werden, bedeutet ihre Arbeit eine Konfrontation. Tatsächlich macht die starke Verbindung zur Geschichte und Tradition der Landschaftsarchitektur und der Kunst die Ausdruckskraft der Arbeiten von Schwartz aus. Anderenfalls wäre sie nur noch eine Künstlerin, die ihren Blick auf ein neues Gebiet richtet, ohne über dessen Traditionen informiert zu sein—wie etwa Mary Miss oder Elyn Zimmerman. Stattdessen verankern Schwartzens explizite Bezugnahmen zur Tradition der Gartengestaltung sie unumstößlich in den Gebieten der Kunst und des Landschaftsdesigns und deren Überschneidungspunkt.

Wie äußern sich diese Bezüge zu den Tradtionen in der Landschaftsarchitektur? Zu erwähnen sind der Auszug und die Veränderung von Elementen französischer Gärten des 17. Jahrhunderts in Projekten wie dem Bagel Garten, dem Necco Garten, dem Splice Garten des Whitehead Instituts und dem King County Jailhouse Garten. Diese Abgrenzungen, Verzierungen und Blumenbeete werden von Antoine-Joseph d'Agenville Dezallier in seiner Abhandlung La Théorie et la Practique du Jardinage (1709) ebenso glaubhaft beschrieben, wie von einem Künstler des späten 20. Jahrhunderts.[14] Diese französische Gartenabhandlung beschreibt die Stadien eines Blumenbeetentwurfes, das Bauzeichnen auf Papier und dann die Übertragung des Designs auf den Boden mit Hilfe von Markierpfosten und Fäden: Techniken, die in der photographischen Dokumentation der vorübergehenden Necco Garten Installation auf dem MIT- Universitätsgelände wiedergegeben wurden. Die Neuentdeckung, die mit diesen historischen Zitaten gekoppelt ist, dreht sich um die Wiedergabe dieser Formen mit unerwarteten Materialien: Plastik, Reifen, Bonbons und zerbrochene Keramikfliesen. Das Vertraute unbekannt machen. Das Alltägliche verwandeln.

Von Zeit zu Zeit löst diese Art von Gartengestaltung Assoziationen aus, die den Besitzer wie den Kritiker stutzig machen. Was sollen wir von den vergoldeten Fröschen halten, die den Drahtglobus im Rio Einkaufszentrum anstarren? Vielleicht sind sie die billigsten Gartenornamente, die man in Atlanta bekommen kann. Zumal sie aber in einem Wasserbasin sitzen und eine ausstrahlende Beziehung zwischen ihnen und dem Globus besteht, ist man geneigt, Vergleiche mit dem Latona Brunnen in Versailles anzustellen, wo eine Gruppe Frösche mit offenem Maul auf konzentrisch angeordneten Steinanhäufungen hockt. Die zentrale Statue, die sich über dem runden Wasserbecken und den Fröschen erhebt, stellt Latona und Jupiters Kinder dar, Diana und Apollo der zukünftige "Sonnenkönig".[15] Der Sage zufolge sind die Frösche Bauern gewesen, die der König zur Strafe für ihr respektloses sich Lustigmachen über Latona und Jupiters Kinder in niedere Amphibien verwandelt hat. Wer hat sich über Schwartz lustig gemacht und warum sind sie zu lebenslänglicher Anbetung des Kudzuglobus verdammt? Oder, wen veralbert Schwartz hier? Die Kritiker, die sagen dies sei keine Landschaftsarchitektur und die ihre eigene Geschichte nicht gut genug kennen, um einen guten Gartenscherz erkennen zu können?

Weitere Aspekte der Arbeit von Schwartz, beispielsweise ihre Dachgärten, verbinden sie mit Designern des frühen zwanzigsten Jahrhunderts, wie Guevrekian und Le Corbusier. Besonders der Surrealismus und die Objektivierung der Natur im Splice Garten Projekt rufen Erinnerungen an Guevrekians Experimente der 20er und 30er Jahre wach. Guevrekians Terrassengarten der Villa Noailles in Hyeres, Frankreich war eine Art Ikone der frühen, modernistischen Landschaftsarchitekten. Fletcher Steeles Veröffentlichung dieses Gartens in der amerikanischen Presse riß das gesammte Feld der Architektur aus seiner Beaux-Art-Selbstzufriedenheit. Neben seiner Schockierrolle hat der Guevrekian Garten mit Schwartzens Dachgärten folgendes gemein. Beide untersuchen die Beziehung zwischen vorausgesetzter und begrifflicher Ordnung mittels Verschiebung des Untergrundes und der damit verbundenen perspektivischen Struktur. Das Ergebnis ist eine Oberfläche, die zwischen der Horizontalen und der Vertikalen onduliert, die den Gartenbesucher in ihre optische und erfahrbare Spielerei hineinzieht. Diese Taktik ist im Splice Garten angewendet, wo die Kunstrasenoberfläche und die Rankengewächse sich vom Boden an der Wand hinauf bis zur Dachkante ausdehnen. Dieser surrealistische Aspekt des Splice Gartens, in dem Formen übertriebene Dimensionen annehmen und an merkwürdigen Orten auftauchen, kommt der Spielerei einer der Le Corbusier Beistegui Dachgärten in Paris sehr nahe. Die dritte Stellungnahme, die Schwartzens Arbeit in der Tradtion der Garten- und Landschaftsgestaltung verankert, beruht auf ihrer immer deutlicher werdenden Tendenz, den Untergrund durch bildhauerisches Behandeln der Erde zu formen. Obwohl man geneigt ist Noguchi, Smithson und Heizer als ihre Vorläufer zu erwähnen, sollte man weder die japanische Tradition des Hügelformens ignorieren, noch die zeitgenößischen Unternehmungen von James Rose, Garrett Eckbo und A.E. Bye. Schwartzens emphatische Erdskulpturen sind umso wirkungsvoller, da sie sich an Orten befinden, die von der zeitgenössischen Architektur als unsichtbar abgetan wurden. Der Federal Courthouse-Platz in Minneapolis ist durch einen Ansammlung eiformiger Hügel aufgeteilt und formiert, die eine Art bewegte Maserung erstellen, als auch eine Art sekundäre Größenordnung für den Platz liefern. In Schwartzens Zusammenarbeit mit Rem Koolhaas am Kunsthal Museumspark in Rotterdam, formt sie die horizontale Ebene als einen schimmernd schwarzen, eiförmigen Hügel, der sich aus einem großen Wasserbasin erhebt. Hier wird Koolhaases Interesse an Größenverhältnissen und der Gegenüberstellung von Größeneinheiten der zeitgenößischen städtischen Umgebung von einer ausdrücklich skulpturellen Landschaftsgegenwart untermauert. Auf dem World Trade Towers Platz verkünden runde Vertiefungen die Unmöglichkeit eine Landschaft herzustellen, die diese Riesen visuell tragen könnte. Der Entwurf ist auf subtilste Weise ausgeführt: eine Serie sich verkleinernder, in den Raum eingelassener Schalen, beinahe unwahrnehmbar, außer wenn sie mit Wasser gefüllt sind. Dann formieren sie ein Feld von Pfützen, die ebenmäßig über den Platz verteilt sind.

Bei zwei Projekten wird die Manipulation des Untergrundes zur symbolischen Dimension. Das Neueste, der Westshore und Rash Field Park in Baltimore, besteht aus einem von schmalen Pfaden durchschnittenen, ondulierenden Grasfeld. Als Ganzes betrachtet fügen sich die Hügel zu einer blauen Krabbe zusammen, eine Delikatesse für die Baltimore und die Chesapeake Bucht sehr bekannt ist. An Kitsch grenzend repräsentiert diese Erd-Krabbe als populare Ikone die Kultur der Region. Auf dem Weg ein Insider Scherz zu werden, allgemein bekannt und von Flugzeugen, die über den inneren Hafen fliegen aus betrachtet, gelingt es der blauen Krabbe einen Ort lebendig zu machen, eine Landschaft aus ihrer anonymen Unsichtbarkeit und Leere zu erretten. Weniger witzig, aber ebenso Stellung nehmend, ist der längliche, brotförmige Haufen, den Schwartz für den Holocaust Denkmals Wettbewerb in Boston vorschlug. Dieser 350 Fuß lange, 12 Fuß hohe Berg aus Betonblöcken hat gleichzeitig irdenen als auch industriellen Charakter. Die plumpe Form scheint aus dem Boden hervor zu brechen, eine von Autos und Touristen umwimmelte längliche Substanz.

Die Gesamtheit des Denkmals wird jedoch zunichte gemacht, indem es aus tausenden von kleinen Einzelteilen konstruiert ist. Es ist gleichzeitig etruskische Grabstätte und Verbrennungsofen des Konzentrationslagers, ein Platz des Friedens und des Unfriedens, Friedhof und Verbrennungsanlage. Es ist eine Einheit, eine Multiplikation von Einzelteilen. Es ist ein Ort des Horrors, eine postmoderne Version des Sublimen. Das Projekt hallt von Bedeutsamkeit wieder, die durch Bilder der Massenkultur, als auch aus der Geschichte der Landschaftsarchitektur bekannte Formen und Typologien, vermittelt wird.

Die Aussagekraft der gebauten und spekulativen Landschaften von Martha Schwartz entspringt ihrer Natur der Kreuzung. Ihre Projekte sind mit formalen und ikonographischen Stellungnahmen zu den Konventionen und Traditionen der Gartengestaltung versehen. Dennoch sind sie vornehmlich von einer Künstlerin und Verbraucherin der Massenkultur entworfen, die den Wert und die Bedeutung des Fertigproduktes erkennt.

Landschaft als Symbol und Bild

Das Werk der Martha Schwartz wirft die Frage auf, wie und wen Landschaftsdesign ansprechen soll. Es erstaunt nicht, daß ihr Werk schwer verständlich ist, wenn man ihre vielseitige Betätigung in den Bereichen der Kunst und der Landschaftsarchitektur, der Massenkultur und der hohen Kultur, der Permanenz und der Vergänglichkeit, des Witzes und der Tiefe betrachtet. Wie dieses Essay durch einige Beispiele zu zeigen versucht, ist es einen Interpretationsversuch wert. Dieses Arbeitsvolumen, das gerade das Stadium der beruflichen Reife erreicht, "bietet sich als Spiegel"[16] für die im Bereich der Landschaftsarchitektur Tätigen an. Darin reflektiert sich vieles der Formlosigkeit und Seichtheit des Berufes. Schwartzens Arbeit versucht nicht einfach nur die Landschaft sichtbar zu machen, sondern sie mit Sinn zu beleben. Schwartzens Landschaftsarbeit richtet sich gegen den Impuls der Architektur einen leeren Raum vorauszusetzen, ihn gewissermaßen zu räumen, bevor man mit dem Entwerfen beginnt. Ihre Projekte fordern von Architekten, daß sie ihre Bauten zur Kommunikation mit ihrer Umgebung öffnen, insbesondere mit der Basis, der Ebene auf der sich das Leben abspielt. Für diejenigen außerhalb dieser beiden Designergebiete, zeigt Schwartzens ungeklärte Position zwischen Kunst und Landschaftsarchitektur wie seicht vieles ist, das dazu beiträgt ein Fachgebiet zu verunsichern. Viele dieser Arbeiten sind eine Art fachfremden Übertritts auf ein neues Gebiet ohne Ahnung von seinen Traditionen, Konventionen, Sprachen oder Bräuchen zu haben. Schwartzens Arbeit bietet ein Alternative, einen Kreuzungsakt, der seine Form und Bedeutung von zwei verschiedenen Denkrichtungen und Praxen bezieht, mit der Absicht weder die eine zu verändern, noch die andere neu auszurichten. Sie benutzt diese schwierige Position, um die Rolle der Landschaft in der heutigen Konsumgesellschaft neu zu definieren.

Ein von Martha Schwartz und ihren Kollegen entwickeltes Projekt fordert nicht nur unsere Wahrnehmung heraus: es rüttelt an unseren Denkmustern. So wie Danto die Wirkung der Brillo Boxes zusammenfaßt, können wir an die Landschaften aus Bagels, Neccos, vergoldeten Fröschen, Kunstgras, Blumenbeeten, verformten New York City Laternen und Bänken und Erd-Krabben herangehen. "Sie leisten das, was Kunstwerke immer geleistet haben: eine Weltanschauung von innen nach außen kehren, das Innenleben einer kulturellen Epoche ausdrücken, sich als Spiegel aufzustellen, um das Gewissen unserer Könige darin einzufangen."[17] Für andere Landschaftsarchitekten heben Schwartzens Projekt die konzeptionellen Strukturen hervor, durch die sie ihr Fach definieren. Sie zeigen derzeitige Begrenzungen und neue Richtungen und Möglichkeiten auf.

Martha Schwartz hat gesagt, daß nicht alles ein Meisterwerk sein muß—ausdauernd, zeitlos und ehrewürdig. Was meint sie damit? Für gewisse Arbeiten ist es ausreichend, einfach Mittel der Landschaftsrepräsentation für die Öffentlichkeit, den Kunden oder Gutachter zu sein. Das Designangebot als Re-Präsentation, als eine Wundertüte oder ein Claude Glass des späten zwanzigsten Jahrhunderts etabliert einen Rahmen der Wertschätzung von vergänglichen Installationen, Gemeinplätzen, vernachlässigten Orten und Randgebieten und der Verwendung gewöhnlicher Materialien und Dinge. Es ermöglicht anderen das Erkennen der Landschaft aus einer neuen Perspektive, die weniger in die ideale, unnahbare Natur verliebt ist und die stattdessen die wahre Landschaft mit all ihren Schönheitsfehlern akzeptiert. Je mehr Kommissionen Schwartz für permanente, öffentliche Einrichtungen bekommt, desto häufiger fragt man sich, ob es nicht vielleicht möglich sei künstlerischen Ausdruck, kulturelle Kritik, rhetorische Gestik in die Schaffung eines Raumes, eines Meisterwerkes zu integrieren. Meisterwerk bedeutet heute soviel wie eine schöne Komposition für einen wohlhabenden Bauherrn, aus dauerhaftem Material, aber leider ohne Inhalt oder Aussage. Kann eine sich der Verwandlung von Gemeinplätzen widmende Praxis, die in der Öffentlichkeit und in Randgebieten baut, zur Schaffung von Meisterwerken emporsteigen?

Martha Schwartz hat 15 Jahre der Experimente, zeitweiliger Installationen, kleiner Aufträge und treuer Kunden zu verzeichnen. Eine Rückschau auf dieses Arbeitsvolumen als Ganzes zeigt seine Wirkung als kulturelle Kritik eindeutiger, als die rhetorischen Gesten einzelner Projekte. Skulpturell in Plastik, Beton und massengefertigten Teilen arbeitend hat diese Praxis als Kulturkritik dem Berufsfeld einen Aktionsplan für die rauhen, komerziellen Landschaften des Einkaufsstreifens, der Verkehrsstraßen und der Vorstädte geliefert. Gibt es im späten 20. Jahrhundert ein Territorium, das im ersatztraditionellen Städtetum nicht vorgesehen war und sich in großer Not zur Verschönerung befindet, so ist es mit Sicherheit die Vorstadtausdehnung mit ihren Parkplätzen, Einkaufszentren, Schnell-Imbissen und kastenförmigen Ladenstraßen und Wohnhausreihen, der Ort wo die meisten Amerikaner leben. Da uns das Problem dieser Alltäglichkeit nun bekannt, aus der Grauzone ans Licht gezerrt worden ist, wird es hoffentlich andere geben, die sich Martha Schwartzens Richtung anschließen. Die Verfasserin meint, daß es an der Zeit ist, ihren substantiellen, kritischen und konstruierten Beitrag zur amerikanischen Landschaft und Landschaftsarchitektur anzuerkennen, statt sie weiterhin als Schänderin von Andachtsbildern, als Einzelgängerin und Zerstörerin des Fachgebietes zu sehen.

Anerkennung:

Während der letzten 8 Jahre habe ich meine Ansichten über zeitgenössische Landschaftsarchitektur gemeinsam mit meinen Studenten zunächst an der Harvard Universität und jetzt an der Universität von Virginia ausgearbeitet. Ich schulde ihnen Dank für ihre enthusiastische und differenzierende Resonanz. Die Forschungsarbeiten und schriftlichen Abhandlungen meiner Studenten haben mir geholfen, meine Auffassung von bestimmten Designern zu ändern oder zu klären.Insbesondere haben Ingrid Cook, Kevin Rasmussen, Alison Ingram und Eric Chou meine Schätzung der Martha Schwartz Entwürfe für das Rio Einkaufszentrum, den Splice Garten und CIT vertieft. Schließlich möchte ich Kaki Martin von der Firma Martha Schwartz danken für die großzügige Hilfe in der Form von verbalen und graphischen Beschreibungen ihrer Projekte.

Anmerkungen:

1 Aus einem öffentlichen Vortrag von Martha Schwartz, dem sog. Myles Thaler Memorial Lecture an der Universität von Virginia School of Architecture in Charlottesville, Virginia (April 1995).

2 Arthur C. Danto, *The Transfiguration of the Commonplace: A Philosophy of Art* (1981), S. 208.

3 J. B. Jackson, "The Word Itself." In *Discovering the Vernacular Landscape* (1984), S. 1-8.

4 Ebenda, S. 8.

5 Denis Cosgrove und Stephen Daniels, "Introduction: Iconography and landscape." In *The Iconography of Landscape* (1988), S. 1.

6 Danto, S. 95.

7 Danto, S. 98.

8 Martha Schwartz, Inc., project descriptions, 1995, S. 37.

9 "Der Glaube an einer 'großen Wasserscheide' (Great Divide) mit ihren ästhetischen, moralischen und politischen Implikationen dominiert noch heute im akademischen Diskurs… Diese These wird aber durch die jüngsten Tendenzen in der Kunst, Literatur und in der kritischen Theorie zunehmend in Frage gestellt. Diesen zweiten großen Angriff in diesem Jahrhundert gegen die im Kanon bestehenden Dichotomie des 'hoch/niedrig' bezeichnet man allgemein als die Postmoderne. Wie die historische Avantgarde (jedoch mit ganz anderen Mitteln), negiert auch die Postmoderne die Theorie und Praxis der 'Great Divide'. . . . Die Grenzen zwischen der hohen Kunst und der Massenkultur sind zunehmend undeutlich geworden, und wird sollten diesen Prozeß als neue Gelegenheit wahrnehmen, statt ihn als Feigheit oder Qualitätsschwund zu lamentieren," Andreas Huyssen, *After the Great Divide* (1986), S. viii-ix.

10 Als Doktorandin an der Universität von Virginia entwickelte Frau Sigrid Cook diese Fragestellung in ihrer Arbeit über Schwartz's Schaffen. Der Aufsatz erschien in *Critiques of Built Work* (1995).

11 Diese Brunnenikonographie kommt in manchen Darstellungen von Versailles zur Sprache. Siehe dazu Hamilton Hazelhurst's *Gardens of Illusion* und Jacques Girard's *Versailles Gardens: Sculpture and Mythology*.

12 Danto, S. 208.

13 Danto, S. 208.

Interview mit Martha Schwartz

Martha Schwartz ist für ihre kurzlebigen Fertigprodukte, Leuchtfarbe und unkonventionell geometrische Muster bekannt. Damit hat sie ein Berufsfeld schockiert, das stark im Erbe von Frederick Law Olmsted verankert ist. Schwartz gelingt es Landschaften zu entwerfen, die mit jedem Auftrag herausfordernder, ironischer und erfinderischer werden. Hier spricht sie über die Einflüsse, auf denen ihre Arbeit für private öffentliche und Firmenklienten basiert.

Sie sind für die Verwendung ungewöhnlicher Materialien in Ihren Landschaften bekannt. Können Sie die Wahl Ihrer Materialien erläutern?

Anfangs stammten meine Materialien aus meinem Interesse an der Popkunst. Ich fühlte mich von der subversiven Qualität minderwertiger Materialien und weggeworfener Objekte angezogen. Ich fand Kunst wie Jasper Johns Glühbirne aus Bronze anziehend—diese unerwartete Zusammmenstellung des Alltäglichen mit dem Besonderen. Die Erhöhung alltäglicher Gegenstände war eine Gegenbewegung in der Kunst, die mich faszinierte.

Ich bewunderte Andy Warhols Brillo-Boxes und seine Forderung, Kunst neu zu definieren. Zu jener Zeit waren die meisten davon überzeugt, daß Brillo Boxes nicht ins Museum gehörten. Ich glaubte, daß man gegen die Regeln im Kunst-Establishment verstoßen konnte und sollte. Aus demselben Grunde war ich an den Erdarbeitskünstlern interessiert: ihre Arbeit war konzeptionell und raumbezogen; sie konnte nicht von der Welt der Gallerien verwässert werden. Ich wollte konventionelles Denken schon herausfordern, als ich von der Existenz der Landschaftsarchitektur noch gar nichts wußte.

Als ich das Studium der Landschaftsarchitektur begann, wurde mir klar, daß der Beruf großen Wert auf die Überlieferung von Handwerk, Tradition und den Gebrauch hochwertiger Materialien legt. Ich fand, daß der Schwerpunkt zu sehr auf Handwerk und Material lag, und daß die Beschäftigung mit, oder ein Interesse an, den konzeptionellen Aspekten der Arbeit völlig fehlte. In der Kunst ist der Begriff Mittelpunkt der Arbeit; in der Landschaftsgestaltung ist es aber die Funktion.

Ich dachte, daß das Fehlen der Ausrichtung auf Konzepte und Ideen mit der Konzentration auf Material und Handwerk zusammenhing. Vielleicht war die Landschaftsarchitektur imstande sich weiterzuentwickeln, wenn wir ermutigt würden zu erweitern, was allgemein unter Materialien verstanden wird. Wir könnten unsere Fachsprache ausbauen; Granitbordsteine könnten mit wiederverwendetem Plastik, Glass, Murmeln oder Kunstgras ersetzt werden. In der Sprache begrenzt unser Wortschatz, was wir eigentlich denken können. In gewisser Weise beschränkte das Fehlen materialmäßiger Möglichkeiten das konzeptionelle Denken in der Landschaftsarchitektur.

Die Erhöhung von Materialien, die mit der Massenkultur assoziiert werden, war damals meine Devise. Inzwischen bin ich aber die Königin des Niedrigbudgets geworden. Ich habe noch nie ein Projekt ausgeführt bei dem ich hätte Steinplatten verwenden können. Meine Entwürfe bestehen aus relativ billigen Materialien, weil meine Kunden sich teure Projekte nicht leisten können. Ich habe mir einen Namen geschafft, indem ich sagte: Sie können keine $40 pro Quadrat Fuß ausgeben, also werden wir etwas mit Integrität und Vorzug für $7 herstellen. Wir werden fertiggegossenen Beton oder Asphalt verwenden und das als etwas Positives betrachten.

Wie reagieren Ihre Klienten, wenn Sie dieses billige Baumaterial empfehlen?

Die veränderte Realität ist die des verschwindenden Rohstoffs. Die Fähigkeit etwas Bemerkenswertes aus einfachen Mitteln zu machen steht nicht länger zur Wahl, sondern ist zur Notwendigkeit geworden. Ich werde häufig gefragt, warum ich Material auswähle, das repariert oder ersetzt werden muß. Die Menschen glauben, wir Künstler und Designer hätten freie Hand in der Wahl unserer Materialqualität. In Wirklichkeit bestimmt aber das Budget des Kunden, das was passiert. Mir steht die Frage, "Was ist Ihnen diese Landschaft wert? Soll sie 100 Jahre oder nur einen Nachmittag halten?" gar nicht zu. Diese Werte sind in der Summe reflektiert, die für ein Projekt ausgegeben wird—ein ganz einfacher Maßstab. Ich kann versuchen, Leute davon zu überzeugen ihren Wertmaßstab zu ändern, aber ich mache keine Budgets. Ich reagiere auf sie.

Im Allgemeinen wird in unserem Land die Landschaft oder der öffentliche Raum nicht geschätzt. Die Verwendung billiger Materialien ist eine Wiederspiegelung dieser Tatsache. Ich versuche, Geist in einen ungeschätzten oder unterbewerteten Raum zu bringen und eine Umgebung mit Zauber und Sinn zu bereichern, und damit zu überspielen, daß ihr Besitzer nur $7 pro Quadrat Fuß auszugeben bereit ist. Das ist weniger als ein durchschnittlicher Teppichpreis.

Es ist unumgänglich, den Wert einfacher, billiger Materialien zu begreifen, wenn man einigermaßen optimistisch in die Zukunft schauen will. Die Welt wird sich nicht rückwärts zum zentralisierten Wohlstand oder zur Tradition des Handwerkertums entwickeln. Wir werden nicht zum Bildhauern aus Stein zurückgreifen. Der Abbau des Handwerks ist ein Resultat der Demokratisierung, der Verteilung des Wohlstandes auf alle. Wir leben in einer Zeit, wo jeder mit einem kleineren Stückchen Kuchen zufrieden sein muß.

Viele der Entscheidungen bezüglich Material reflektieren heute ein Maß an kultureller Unehrlichkeit. Ich werde immer wieder damit konfrontiert. Die Kunden fühlen sich häufig mit Materialien niedriger Qualität nicht wohl, sind aber weder bereit, noch in der Lage, das Budget zu erhöhen und ihrem Standard anzupassen. Das führt zu dem, was ich das "Furnier Problem" nenne. Ein Kunde deutet an, daß er das Aussehen beispielsweise von Granit haben möchte, was bedeutet, daß er etwas vorgeben will, was nicht existiert. Das Anliegen ist—und ich muß da als Designer mitziehen—etwas Preisgünstiges zu bauen, was eine teuere Illusion kreiert. Solange gegossener Beton das Aussehen von Stein hat, ist das Ziel erreicht.

Ich finde das furchtbar unehrlich. Es liegt mir nichts daran, Leute zu verblöden. Wenn man sich nur Beton leisten kann, dann stellt sich die Frage, wie man diesen Beton zur Schaffung einer Idee anwenden kann. Es sollte ein Ausdrucksmittel sein, nicht ein Mittel zur Vortäuschung oder Selbsttäuschung. Ich meine, ein wahres Design oder Kunstwerk besitzt Integrität.

Kunst ist die Erforschung des Wesentlichen, rein oder elementar, denn die Wiedergabe einer Gemütsstimmung, eines Gefühls oder einer Idee ist nötig, wenn die Kunst unsere Kultur beeinflussen soll. Je direkter und ehrlicher man in der Aussage ist, desto unmittelbarer ist die Kommunikation. Kunststoff stört mich überhaupt nicht, solange man es nicht als Kunstleder vorgibt. Intellektuelle Unehrlichkeit und Angeberei zeigen uns, daß Menschen nicht damit zufrieden sind, mit dem was sie sind. Wenn ein Designer mit Hilfe von Furnier eine Täuschung erreicht, entfernt uns das vom Verständnis dessen, was und wer wir sind.

Was ist Ihre Antwort auf die Behauptung, Sie seien keine Landschaftsarchitektin, da Sie keine Pflanzen mögen.

Ich benutze Pflanzen, wenn die Situation sie vorsieht. Ich muß wieder betonen, daß viele Leute gar nicht verstehen, welch ein Aufwand es ist, eine Landschaft zu kreieren, besonders in einer Vorstadtsituation. Um eine Landschaft auf einem Garagendach oder auf einer Terasse zu bauen, muß für das erhöhte Gewicht Stahl eingelassen werden; solche Konstruktionen sind teuer. Und dann muß sie gepflegt werden. Eine Landschaft anzulegen ist ein ähnliche Entscheidung wie die zu einem Kind oder einem Haustier: wenn nicht genug Geld da ist, um es richtig zu machen, dann sollte man es lassen. Wenn in unseren Projekten keine Pflanzen vorkommen, bedeutet das meistens, daß das Geld oder die Fähigkeit zur Pflege fehlt.

Sie arbeiten mit einer grellbunten Farbpalette. Können Sie uns etwas über die Farbverwendung in Ihren Landschaftsdesigns erzählen?

Schon als kleines Mädchen habe ich bunte Farben geliebt. Es ist wie die Liebe zu Bonbons. Eine meiner Großmütter hatte eine kindliche Vorliebe für Farben. Sie brachte mir immer knallig bunte Mitbringsel aus Florida mit, und sie hatte das ganze Jahr über Gipsenten und Plastikblumen in ihrem Garten. Wenn alle anderen Gärten grau und verschneit waren, hatte sie dort Gruppen wunderschöner, farbiger Blumen. Als kleines Mädchen kritisierte ich ihre Gärten nicht als unnatürlich oder geschmacklos —wir sind hier im trüben, nordöstlichen Philadelphia. Ich freute mich an diesen Farben genauso wie sie. Ich habe es immer geliebt, Farben zu betrachten. Ich habe mir nie erlaubt, aus dieser Begeisterung heraus zu wachsen. Es ist wichtig, einige kindlichen Qualitäten in uns zu beschützen. Es regt mich immer noch an, frohe Farben zu sehen, und zwar sehen sie draußen noch besser aus, als drinnen.

Wenn wir erwachsen werden, lernen wir, was in den Augen anderer geschmackvoll und akzeptabel ist. Wir lernen uns von der Palette der lauten, grellen Farben und des Glitters aus unserer Kinderzeit nicht mehr animieren zu lassen. Das ganze Thema des Geschmackvollen widert mich an. Geschmack ist eine Reihe von Regeln, die diktieren wie man aussehen, handeln und fühlen soll. Unsere Kultur hat auch eine Art Farbphobie. Das Fehlen von Farbe in unserer Kultur entstammt dem nordeuropäischen Einfluß. Wenn Menschen frohe Farben sehen, sind sie oft begeistert und erleichtert. Es signalisiert ihnen, Erlaubnis zu freierem Benehmen. Es ist bezeichnend wie wirkungsvoll eine Signalfarbe sein und eine Stimmung vermitteln kann.

Welche Landschaftsarchitekten sind Ihre Vorbilder?

Meine wichtigste Inspiration bezog ich von der Arbeit Isamu Noguchis. Als ich mit meinem Studium begann, war ich von seinen horizontalen Erdformierungen sehr beeinflußt und auch von seinen Bühnenbildern für Martha Graham. Noguchi überwindet die Trennung zwischen Kunst, Design und Landschaftsarchitektur. Seine Landschaften schaffen magische, surreale Orte.

Sie haben geschrieben, daß die Kunst der Landschaftsarchitektur die Beziehung zwischen Natur und Kultur definieren wird. Können Sie das näher erläutern?

Ich benutze die Landschaft als Aussage darüber, was es bedeutet, Mensch zu sein und Ideen zu haben. Die Landschaften, die mir am besten gefallen sind die, die Aspekte unserer Menschlichkeit anerkennen und wiedergeben. Eine großartige Landschaft anzuschauen ist wie in einen Spiegel zu sehen oder ein Porträt zu betrachten.

Viele Leute denken sofort an die Natur wenn sie den Begriff Landschaftsarchitektur hören. Natürliche Landschaften spielen in unserer Kultur eine große Rolle. Mich interessiert die konstruierte und bewohnte Landschaft am meisten. Ich frage mich bei meiner Arbeit immer, "wie reflektiert die Landschaft, wer wir sind und wer wir sein wollen?"

Ich habe immer gerne lebendige Dinge unserem Nutzen untergeordnet. Es fasziniert mich, Außenräume als bewohnbare Räume zu nutzen. Landschaften in denen Bäume Gänge formieren, Rankenpflanzen zu Hütten und Hecken zu Räumen werden mich beeindrucken. Ich bin begeistert von diesen traditionellen Orten, die weder Natur noch Architektur sind.

Ich bin in Philadelphia aufgewachsen. Wir gingen oft zu den Longwood Gardens, um diese unglaublichen Treibhäuser zu besuchen in denen es formale Gärten mit Böden aus Gras gab. Ich träumte davon in einem Haus zu leben, wo meine Füsse sofort einen Teppich aus Gras berührten, wenn ich morgens aufstand. Ich glaube nicht, daß es destruktiv ist, die Natur unseren Bedürfnissen anzupassen, vor allem wenn man den Menschen als Teil der Natur sieht. Ich meine, daß man Städte, Häuser und Räume—Plätze zum Essen und Entspannen, Plätze zum Leben—aus Landschaften bauen kann und soll.

Ihre Liebe zur Natur ist die zur eingerahmten Natur. Was empfinden sie für einen Ort wie beispielsweise den Yosemite Park?

Für mich ist die Schönheit einer Idee gleichwertig der Schönheit der Natur. Ich werde durch die Kraft und Schönheit von Ideen beflügelt. Ich liebe Städte: sie sind die Aufbewahrungsstätten der Kultur. Ich bin stärker beeindruckt von dem, was ich in New York City sehen und hören kann, als dem was es in Yosemite zu sehen und zu hören gibt.

Aber ich würde niemals sagen, daß Wildnis unwichtig ist. Ich meine sie ist auf abstrakte Weise wichtig. Wir müssen alle wissen, daß die Wildnis existiert und daß sie erreichbar wäre, wenn wir sie nötig hätten. Sehr wenige von uns erleben heute noch echte Wildnis— für die meisten Amerikaner ist sie eine abstrakte Vorstellung. Um zur Wildnis zu gelangen muß man sich anstrengen, in ein Flugzeug steigen, dann ein Auto. Dann ist man kurz da, und dann geht man wieder weg. Ich frage mich, ob wir nicht vielleicht mit einer praktischen Form von Wildnis auskommen könnten—auf einem Computerbildschirm oder durch ein virtual reality Modum. In der Wildnis zu sein ist eine weitaus abstraktere Erfahrung, als in einer Großstadt oder Vorstadt zu leben. Die Wildnis ist eine romantische Phantasie, aber nicht Teil unserer Realität.

Leider hat der Widerstand gegenüber Landschaftsarchitektur größtenteils mit der Wildnisphantasie der Amerikaner zu tun. Während wir uns einbilden in schönster Wildnis zu leben, haben wir viel Häßliches sich über unsere Landschaft ausbreiten lassen. Wir sind von unserer Wildnisidee so verblendet, daß alles, was nicht Wildnis ist einfach links liegen gelassen wird. Da ein Einkaufszentrum keine Wildnis ist, verdient seine Umgebung keine besondere Beachtung. Es ist akzeptabel sie zu einem Parkplatz ohne Bäume zu degradieren. Der Gedanke, daß der Parkplatz eines Einkaufszentrums ein interessantes, landschaftliches Potential sein könnte, ist dem Amerikaner noch nicht gekommen. Wir haben nicht das Geld, die Gesetze oder die Zeit und Kraft Landschaft und Parkmöglichkeiten als Einheit zu konzipieren.

Sie haben geschrieben, daß unsere Landschaft so behandelt wird, wie die Frauen in der viktorianischen Zeit, d.h. entweder als Jungfrau oder als Hure.

Das stimmt. Menschen neigen dazu, die Landschaft in ihrer Vorstellung zu zerteilen. Landschaft wird hauptsächlich als reines Überbleibsel der Natur verstanden. "Landschaft existiert in Parkanlagen und in Yosemite. Der Gedanke, daß Landschaft in Form von Parkplätzen, Hausdächern und Mittelstreifen vorkommt, ist schwer zu akzeptieren. Der Begriff "Natur" umschreibt malerische Visionen. Wenn sie nicht malerisch oder natürlich ist, lassen wir unsere Landschaften urteilslos verkommen. Wir haben noch gar keinen Namen für die Landschaften gefunden, die wir als Lebensraum um uns herum haben entstehen lassen.

Gibt es Kulturen, die mit der Frage der Schaffung öffentlicher Landschaften besser umgehen?

Die Kulturen von Frankreich, Deutschland, Holland, Spanien, Japan und Italien sind uns weit voraus. Unser Versagen ist deshalb so enttäuschend, weil wir wohlhabend und fähig sind. Viele Länder hungern so sehr nach allgemeiner Entwicklung, daß ihr Vergessen der Landschaftsfrage, obwohl bedauerlich, verständlich ist. Es ist schwer Menschen dazu zu bringen, auf ökologisch verantwortliche oder schöne Weise zu bauen, wenn sie Förderung, Arbeitsstellen und Handel brauchen.

Wir hingegen sollten etwas weitsichtiger in Bezug auf unsere Landschaft sein. Wir haben die Mittel Umfelder zu schaffen, die mit unserer Lebensweise im Einklang stehen. Ich meine damit Umgebungen, die unsere städtische, vorstädtische und ländliche Landschaft gleichermaßen betrifft. Länder wie Frankreich und Holland sind sehr fortschrittlich in ihrem Verständnis von der Landschaft als Raum, der menschliche Nutzung voraussetzt und auf sie reagiert.

Was machen die Landschaftskünstler und -designer in diesen Ländern anders?

Aus Holland kommen heute die weltweit fähigsten Landschaftsarchitekten. Die Holländer haben einen Vorsprung, da sie ihre Landschaft sozusagen von Grund auf hergestellt haben. Teile ihres bewohnten Landes sind ja dem Ozean abgewonnen. Sie trauern keiner Phantasie von der unberührten, unverdorbenen Wildnis nach. Sie sind freier in ihrem Denken über das Manipulieren ihrer Landschaft, da sie teilweise von vorn herein menschlicher Konstruktion entstammt.

In den meisten europäischen Großstädten sind die Wohngegenden, z. B. Verkehrsstraßen und Zuggleisen, viel schöner als unsere. Diese Länder unterstützen ihre Künstler und Designer, was zeigt, daß diese Kulturen großen Wert auf die Qualität ihrer visuellen Umgebung legen. Die Franzosen identifizieren sich mit ihrer bebauten Umgebung und erkennen sich selbst darin wieder. Wir hingegen tun das nicht. Wir sehen Kunst und Design als Zusatzbehandlung—etwa wie die Kirsche auf dem Kuchen. Wir Amerikaner sehen den Einkaufsstreifen am Rand unserer Städte nicht als Symbol unserer nationalen Identität. Wir identifizieren uns nicht auf diese Art mit der Landschaft. Wir identifizieren uns mit den Phantasiebildern malerischer Landschaften auf Reklametafeln, in Zeitschriften oder im Fernsehen, aber niemals mit unseren tatsächlichen Wohnstätten.

Unsere Straßen, Brücken, Wege, Parkanlagen und unser Verkehrssystem werden als notwendige Umgebung ohne Bedarf oder Raum für Kunst gesehen. Wenn ich aus anderen Ländern heim komme und aus dem Flugzeug steige, erkenne ich jedesmal die enge Auffassung, die wir von der Essenz des Lebens haben. Der Wert der Funktionalität regiert über dem der Schönheit. Wir sind eine Nation von Tiefffliegern; wir haben einen niedrigen Schönheitsbegriff und das zeigt sich rechts und links.

Wie können Sie ein Klima schaffen, das ein Wertschätzung der gebauten Landschaft ermöglicht? Wie können wir lernen, Parkplätzen, Einkaufsstraßen und Grünstreifen Beachtung zu schenken?

Ich bin kein Evangelist, aber ich unterrichte und hoffe, daß das, was ich baue dazu beiträgt, Landschaft sichtbar zu machen, wo sie sonst nicht gesehen wird. Vielleicht kann ich sie dadurch als Experimentierfeld für Designer und Künstler erschließen. Ich habe oft das Gefühl als reagierte ich nur auf den Markt, aber letztendlich erziehe ich meine Kunden doch mit jedem Projekt ein Stückchen weiter in Richtung der endlosen Möglichkeiten, die die Landschaft birgt. Es ist ein langsamer Prozeß.

Es ist sehr schwierig, jemandem etwas über Kunst und Design zu vermitteln, wenn er vorher noch nie damit in Berührung gekommen ist. Viele meiner Kunden sind sehr intelligent und auf den meisten Gebieten bewandert. Oft fehlt ihnen jedoch die Basis zum Verständnis visueller Ideen. Sie haben einfach keinen Einblick in das Thema Kunst. In diesem Land werden Kunst und Kunstgeschichte in der Schule nicht mehr unterrichtet. Wenn man zuhause nicht mit Ästhetik in Berührung gekommen ist, gibt es wenig Chance, so etwas in unserer Kultur nachzuholen. Andere Kulturen tragen einen stärkeren Hang zur Ästhetik in sich. Das allgemeine Fehlen von Verständnis und Unterstützung in den Vereinigten Staaten verursacht für viele Landschaftsarchitekten, Künstler und Architekten ein großes Dilemma. Besteigen wir ein Flugzeug und fliegen nach Japan, weil die Japaner die Rolle der Ästhetik in ihrer Umgebung verstehen? Oder sollten wir versuchen, auch hier Interesse und Unterstützung aufzuwiegeln? Wenn wir uns entscheiden, unsere Arbeit in USA zu leisten, stellt sich die Frage wie in einer Zeit der schwindenden Rohstoffe vorzugehen ist.

In einem Ihrer Vorträge haben Sie Ihren Zuhörern gesagt, daß Sie nach Firmen und Institutionen suchen, die hinter Ihrer Idee der Verbesserung des gebauten Umfeldes stehen. Haben Sie Erfolg gehabt?

Ich habe inzwischen einige öffentliche Aufträge für die GSA (General Services Administration) ausgeführt. Auch in öffentlicher Arbeit braucht man jemanden, der einem beisteht und bereit ist, ein Risiko einzugehen. Leider sind die meisten im öffentlichen Dienst risikounfreudig. Sie werden gewählt und stehen dann zur Wiederwahl an, sie sind nicht autonom. Folglich ist es sehr schwierig, jemanden zu finden, der Ihnen während des gesamten Prozesses zur Seite stehen kann. Man muß jemanden finden, der davon überzeugt ist, daß man als Künstler oder Designer etwas für die Öffentlichkeit wirklich Wichtiges zu sagen hat.

Wir sind dabei, eine Reihe Regierungsprojekte fertig zu stellen: Jacob Javits Platz in Manhattan, der HUD Platz in Washington und der Platz für den neuen Gerichtshof in Minneapolis. Diese Projekte haben große Zukunftschancen. Regierungsprojekte sind dafür bekannt, aussagelos und nicht kontrovers zu sein, was auf die Überzeugung zurückgeht, daß öffentliche Projekte sich einem jeden Benutzer anzupassen haben. Das hat als Folge, daß die Entwürfe, die auf den niedrigsten gemeinsamen Nenner gebracht sind, um politische Probleme zu vermeiden. Für mich sind diese Projekte ein Versuch der Erforschung, ob es möglich ist, interessante und abenteuerliche, öffentliche Werke zu schaffen. Keins dieser Projekte ist teuer. Alles muß aber durch die Gutachten gehen. Wir haben einen aufgeklärten Förderer in der GSA, der aufpaßt, daß dem Schmetterling die Flügel nicht abgerissen werden, daß die künstlerische Absicht eine wesentliche Komponente bleibt.

Haben die GSA Projekte einen gemeinsamen Nenner?

Diese Plätze—Javits, HUD, Minneapolis—sind typisch für Gebäudevorplätze, wie man sie in den 60er Jahren anlegte. Gemäß der modernistischen Lehre jener Zeit hatten Gebäude als heroische, skulpturelle Objekte auf einer leeren, utopischen Ebene zu stehen. Üblicherweise verbannten die Architekten alles in der Nähe des Gebäudes, um jegliche Konkurrenz mit seiner skulpturellen Form zu vermeiden. Leere, von Parkplätzen flankierte, Vorplätze schafften tote Räume am Fuß der Gebäude. Mit der Zeit hat man versucht diese Plätze zu beleben, jedoch ohne großen Erfolg.

Viele unserer wichtigsten Innenstädte sind in der Expansionszeit der 60er Jahre entstanden, als man diese neutralen Plätze konstruierte. Der Postmodernismus hat diese Orte kritisiert. Wir haben erkannt, daß die Häuserfassaden vielleicht doch ihr Gutes haben, daß große, offene Plätze eine Leere erzeugen und daß wir menschliche Umgebungen am Fuß großer Gebäude einrichten sollten. Die Vorrangigkeit des Gebäudes als Skulptur ist in Frage gestellt worden. Eine Überhohlung hat stattgefunden, und es wird der Versuch gemacht diese Orte nachträglich zu integrieren und zu beleben.

Diese drei GSA Projekte reflektieren alle eine trockene, leichtherzige Stimmung. Welche Rolle spielt der Humor in ihren Entwürfen?

Meine ganze Familie hat einen großen Sinn für Humor. Ich entstamme der jüdischer Tradition, wo der Humor ein wirksames Mittel ist, sich mit schmerzhaften Themen zu befassen. Das alte Sprichwort, daß Komödie eine sehr ernste Sache sei, ist absolut wahr. Der Großteil der guten Komödie ist dem Zorn enstanden; mir ist oft aufgefallen, daß Komödianten die ärgerlichsten Menschen sein können. Ich bin auch eine ziemlich ärgerliche Person. Ärger sport mich an. Humor ist eine gesellschaftlich akzeptierte Form, Ärger und Frustration zum Ausdruck zu bringen. Humor hat den Effekt, Menschen zu erweichen, sie empfänglich zu machen. Sie sind froh, wenn sie zum Lachen gebracht werden, denn es wirkt erleichternd.

Bitte erläutern Sie Ihren Entwurf für den Jacob Javits Platz, auf dem bisher Richard Serras "Titled Arch" stand.

Unsere Version des Javits-Platzes ist eine Reaktion auf die Skulptur "Titled Arch". Ich wollte eine Antithese zum "Titled Arch" schaffen—weniger selbstgewichtig und weniger selbstbezogen. Sie ist in ihrer Ambition einfacher: ein einladender Ort zum Hinsetzen und zum Mittag zu essen. Der "Titled Arch" war eine Kritik an modernistischer Architektur und ein Ausdruck der Befremdung. Er war eine starke Konfrontation. Auf unserem Javits-Platz muß man sich nicht auf Konfrontation einlassen, man kann ganz einfach da sein und essen.

Die öffentliche Kunstwelt lernte viel von den Prüfungen des "Titled Arch". Der Nutzen des Raumes war der Vision des Künstlers geopfert worden und die Frage, ob ein solcher Umsturz für öffentliche Kunst angebracht ist, wurde zu einer sehr wertvollen Diskussion. Während dieser Ereignisse kam ich zu einer neuen Einstellung darüber, was öffentliche Kunst leisten sollte. Sie muß auf mehr als einer Ebene bestehen können. Sie befindet sich nicht in einer Gallerie. Folglich kann man sich nicht aussuchen, ob man sich mit ihr befassen will. Die beste öffentliche Kunst hat verschiedene Ebenen der Ansprache und wenn man von ihr unangesprochen bleiben will, ist das auch möglich.

Welchen Rat würden Sie städtischen Behörden zur Verbesserung der Umgebung der Vorstädten geben?

Die meisten öffentlichen Plätze werden ignoriert und mißbraucht, einfach und ärmlich ausgestattet. Es existiert dort gar kein Gefühl von Raum, hauptsächlich deshalb weil keine Risiken eingegangen werden. Es braucht Mut eine Vision zu sanktionieren, aber öffentliche Projekte befinden sich meist unter der Aufsicht öffentlicher Angestellter, die ihrerseits Überprüfungen ausgesetzt sind. Wenn wir Plätze, Parkanlagen, Straßen, Parkplätze und Dächer haben wollen, die weniger anonym sind, ist es unumgänglich, daß die Stadträte mehr von den Designern dieser Orte verlangen. Wir stellen Anforderungen an Architekten, aber Landschaftsarchitektur ist als Kunstform noch nicht erkannt worden. Es ist wichtig, daß öffentliche Angestellte einen höheren Standard setzen und verlangen, daß dies Räume persönlichen Charakter und Geist aufweisen. Um funktional zu sein, muß eine Landschaft von ihren Bewohnern emotional und spirituell angenommen werden.

Können Sie etwas über die psychologischen Auswirkungen der degradierten Landschaft auf den Amerikaner sagen? Sie haben gesagt, unsere Landschaft zu heilen könnte uns dabei helfen, unsere sozialen Krankheiten zu heilen.

Ich glaube, daß unser Lebensumfeld uns im Kern unserer Selbstdefinition trifft und unsere Erwartungen und Hoffnungen beeinflußt. Menschen reagieren von Natur aus auf etwas Schönes. Es ist nichts, waß wir in einem Dia-Vortrag lernen. Menschen reagieren auf die Qualität eines Raumes, auf Proportionen, Farben, Licht, Rhytmus und Oberflächenstruktur. Es bedarf keiner großen Anstrengung, sich den psychologischen Effekt auf jemanden vorzustellen, der von einer Vorstadtwohnung in einen schönen Raum voll Licht und Luft kommt oder von einem Einkaufsstreifen voller Parkplätze auf die Champs Elysees.

Wir neigen dazu uns einzubilden, die Menschen nähmen diese Unterschiede nicht wahr, aber das stimmt nicht. Menschen leben besser an Orten, die besser aussehen und sich besser anfühlen. Wir sind keine Tiere in der Wildnis, wir sind Menschen.

Kunst ist ein Maßstab des Wohlstandes. Wenn in einer Kultur die Kunst floriert, bedeutet dies, daß die Grundbedürfnisse des Lebens abgedeckt sind: Unterkunft, kein Krieg, eine stabile Regierung, Nahrung und ein bestimmtes Maß an Voraussagbarkeit: was macht man wenn für diese Dinge gesorgt ist? Man träumt, schreibt, malt und legt Gärten an. Gartengestaltung ist ein wahrer Luxus, was der Grund ist, warum so wenige Kulturen eine eigene Gartenfachsprache entwickelt haben. Es bedarf einer stabilen, wohlhabenden Kultur, um solche Umgebungen zu kreieren. Meine Frustration ist, daß wir Amerikaner Umgebungen schaffen könnten, die besser für uns sind. Leider entschließen wir uns dagagen.

Können Sie etwas über den Gebrauch der Geometrie in der Landschaft sagen?

Rechtecke und Linien sind menschliche Erfindungen. Wenn wir eine geometrische Ordnung über eine Landschaft legen, infizieren wir sie sozusagen mit menschlichem Denken. Die Geometrie unterscheidet ganz klar eine künstliche von einer natürlichen Umgebung. Wenn man etwas im natürlichen Chaos der Natur erkenntlich machen will, dann ist das wirksamste Mittel dem Ort eine geometrische Ordnung überzustülpen. Geometrie ist auch in der Vorstadtausdehnung vorhanden, Geplante Bauten werden dort in ein vorgefertigtes Gitterschema eingefügt.

Es interessiert mich, menschliche Empfindungen im Räumlichen wiederzugeben. Draußen ist das nicht einfach wegen der weitläufigen Größenordnung der Architektur und wegen der chaotischen Erscheinungsform der Natur. Wir tragen geometrische Formen in unseren Köpfen herum und können uns jederzeit einen Kreis oder ein Rechteck vorstellen. Wenn wir also diese Formen auf dem Boden anwenden, hilft das den Menschen sich auf der Erde zu orientieren. Wenn sie hingegen einer Amöben- oder Naturform gegenüberstehen, mit der sie noch nie in Berührung gekommen sind, wirkt das sehr desorientierend. Man ist einfach nie sicher, wo man ist. Man braucht draußen eine geistig-vertraute Landkarte. *The Citadel* ist beispielsweise eine stark geordnete Landschaft, in der vertraute Formen serienmäßig vorkommen. Diese Wiederholung schafft einen Bezug zum architektonischen Raum und definiert den Raum an sich. Da Räume von Menschen bewohnbar gemacht werden ist der Raum, in dem etwas stattfindet, häufig Thema meiner Arbeiten. Das allein ist schon ein starker Kontrast zur Natur.

Was ist Ihre Definition eines Gartens?

Ein Garten, im Vergleich zur Landschaft, ist ein Ort, der ein Gefühl der Abgeschiedenheit von der Außenwelt vermittelt. Diese Trennung wird durch eine Art Eingangsschwelle—wirklich oder imaginär—erreicht. Diese Schwelle ermöglicht es uns, eine Welt zu verlassen und eine neue zu betreten. Das ist die grundsätzliche Funktion des Gartens: einem Menschen den psychologischen Raum zum Träumen, Denken, Ausruhen und Abschalten zu geben. Er funktioniert als Unterbrechung der täglichen Routine, wie etwa das Betreten einer Kirche oder eines Tempels. Er soll eine Art psychologischen Raum schaffen, der uns auf der Suche nach unserem wahren Selbst behilflich ist.

Was ist die Prognose für die Landschaftsarchitektur in Amerika?

Was die Landschaft uns bedeutet, müssen wir neu definieren. Ich sehe alles als Landschaft an, was außerhalb des Bauplanes existiert—der Weg, die Fahrstraße, der Parkplatz und alle Zwischenräume. Wenn wir sie nur als angrenzend an Architektur verstehen—als Parkanlagen, Gärten und Plätze—wird die Landschaftsarchitektur zum Randberuf. Wir müssen uns darauf konzentrieren brauchbarer zu werden. Wir müssen Projekte annehmen, die weniger Prestigeorientiert sind und damit beginnen, uns mit unserer physisch und visuell zerstörten Landschaft auseinanderzusetzen. Das ist unsere Zukunft. Für wohlhabende Klienten, Gärten zu entwerfen mag sehr befriedigend sein, aber es reicht allein nicht aus, unseren Beruf am Leben zu erhalten.

In einer ausgeglichenen Umgebung zu leben ist von wachsender Bedeutung. Viele meinen jedoch in dem Bestreben, die Landschaft intakt zu halten, sei Design überflüssig. Ich halte das für eine falsche Einstellung, die von unserem Beruf selbst verursacht wurde. Es ist meine Hoffnung, daß die Sensibilität für unsere Umgebung sich eines Tages mit allen visuellen Komponenten unserer bebauten Umgebung auseindersetzen wird. Das wird unsere Rolle sein: intakte, gesunde Umfelder zu kreieren, die gleichzeitig schöne, bedeutungsvolle Orte für ihre Bewohner sind.